TRY
AND
CONVERSION

Glyn Wood

Published by Glyn Wood

Publishing partner: Paragon Publishing, Rothersthorpe

First published 2019

© Glyn Wood, 2019

Some names and identifying details have been changed.

ISBN 978-1-78222-715-1

Book design, layout and production management by Into Print

www.intoprint.net

01604 832149

CONTENTS

"What a great story. Former Rugby star and coach Glyn Wood tells an amazing tale of his life in sport, business and the Royal Navy, including the iconic Field Gun competition at the Royal Tournament. He also weaves fascinating insights from his family life and Christian commitment."

The Rt Rev'd John Holbrook, Bishop of Brixworth

Introduction

I attempt to write this book as someone who is immensely grateful for the abundance of experiences and opportunities afforded me throughout my life. It is only with hindsight that we see our hopes and aspirations come to fruition, giving us an opportunity to acknowledge someone or something for the outplaying of those plans. I pray that I have managed to relay my thanks and gratitude in the best way possible to those who planted good seeds in my life, many of which have flourished, but a majority remain unseen by those who planted them. Most of all I thank Jesus Christ for changing me from what I was to who I hope to be, something that is still a work in progress.

Coming from a working-class background in Sheffield clearly defined who I thought I was or, more to the point, who I thought I should be. It is made significantly easier to accept such a branding when your family are content with their lot, which mine were, but it wasn't until I joined the Royal Navy, aged sixteen, that much of my potential began to unfold.

This is my story of a journey that took me from rags to riches physically, emotionally, financially and, most of all, spiritually. It was a path that started to change for the better when I began to listen with my heart as well as my head, where pride was supplanted with humility, allowing grace (undeserved love or favour) to flourish and to be better understood.

For it is by grace you have been saved, through faith – and this is not from yourselves, it is the gift of God – not by works, so that no one can boast.

Ephesians ch.2, v.8-9

I pray that this book is a source of encouragement and blessing on your life, Amen.

Glyn Wood, July 2019

5

Chapter One

SAINT OR SINNER?

In 1984, a representative from the committee at Northampton Rugby Club told me that I was now a 'Saint,' (the club's nickname) after scoring a try and making my first team debut at No.8, against London Irish. I'd already had the privilege of playing regularly against top clubs for United Services Portsmouth, the Royal Navy, then against Canada and Australia whilst representing the Combined Services. A successful trial for the Saints was the start of a regular commute from Weymouth to play for them. But less than three years later I'd moved on to join Bedford Blues, scoring a try on my debut against Ebbw Vale, just before leaving the Royal Navy as an Aircraft Mechanic and starting a new career as an Estate Agent in the town.

Ten years later, I discovered that I was a real Saint when 'The Holy Bible' told me so, after repenting and asking Jesus Christ to forgive me for my sins. I was thirty-seven years old when my conversion to Christianity took place – a heartfelt, spiritual awakening that was as exciting as anything I've ever done or achieved previously, an adventure and a way of life that I am still working through daily.

These are both true statements that take some living up to, where I was expected to be both a role model and ambassador for my rugby club, and then again as a Christian convert. Rebellion, circumstances, stubbornness or pride have sometimes prevented me from being a 'good role model', and with rugby I was further influenced by the additional pressure to constantly perform at a high level; self-imposed or otherwise. Furthermore, as I got older there was always an assumption that I should dominate my opposite number, never take a step back, and to sort out any problems. In practice, it was scarce for matches to get too out of hand, although intimidation and niggles were prevalent in the game. Even though I always try to do my best, the following stories will determine whether you think me a Saint, Sinner or both…

Some of our thoughts, words and deeds can be considered sinful at times; in fact, Jesus taught that just looking at a woman with wrong motives is adultery. But if we look at it initially as a deliberate act of doing something tangible, that is considered 'wrong,' and that we did it to deliberately hurt someone, then most of us may struggle to pinpoint the first time we ever did such a thing. Perhaps my first hurtful action, that I purposefully initiated, was when I hit my sister's doll on the floor with a view to getting her wound up and tearful, as I can't recall doing anything with malice in my heart before that time. But scripture tells us that we are born into sin, that we need to reconcile ourselves with God and start a new life, and it's one of the reasons so many people opt to have their children baptised at a very young age, many of whom then profess to be a Christian (a follower of Christ). How sad that most of us don't go on to follow Jesus's teaching thereafter, honouring and glorifying Him as our Creator God.

Before my conversion to the Christian faith and making him my priority in life, I would have been at a loss without Rugby Union. It was still an amateur sport but it was the only thing I was ever truly confident in doing, and to have played during the professional era, with experts in coaching, fitness and nutrition supporting me, would have been a dream come true. It was after playing against Canada for the Combined Services in 1983, that my scrum-half teammate asked why I wasn't playing at a senior club, after telling me that I'd walk in to his first team at Northampton. The timely prompt encouraged me to make the effort to test my ability, and within a few weeks I'd completed a successful trial game for the Saints, going on to play thirty-six games for the 1st XV.

Deployment to a ship and being part of the Fleet Air Arm Field Gun Crew throughout most of 1984 limited my first team opportunities, but I was selected to play for the East Midlands in the annual Mobbs Memorial Match versus the Barbarians on two occasions. By 1985, selection for the first team became difficult when a policy was introduced that if you didn't train, then you didn't play, a decision I found frustrating as I lived one-hundred-and-sixty-eight miles away. Nevertheless, I still played occasionally for the first team, but mainly for the 2nd XV whenever I could make it. Winning one of the games against the Barbarians, and featuring on the BBC's Rugby Special programme against Bective Rangers and Nottingham were my most memorable highlights at the club, although a return trip to Dublin to play Bective Rangers holds my attention.

I'd travelled overnight on the mail train from Weymouth, after completing a late shift working at Portland. The journey to Northampton lasted seven-and-a-half hours and it was a most welcome sight to see the 'Super Sausage' transport café open, at just after 6am on the Saturday. One hour later, after making my way across town, I scared the living daylights out of the caretaker of the club, after he found me huddled up and freezing cold in the porchway of the clubhouse. It was a dark January morning and he thought that I was a bag of rubbish. Not only did I look like a sack of spuds, but I felt like a sack of spuds when my team captain appeared and asked why I looked like a tramp, and where was my blazer?

Some hours later we arrived at Dublin Airport and I realised then that I was in trouble. I had forgotten to obtain from naval authorities a special pass that would have allowed me to travel to Ireland, and my passport had my occupation as 'Government Service' imprinted on the inside. It was mooted within the services that some staff at major ports or airports in Ireland would tip off the IRA if forces personnel let slip their identity, and this put the wind up me a little. My concern was short-lived, as it turned out that customs were waiting for the team and allowed us to go through 'en bloc' on the say-so of a committee member identifying us, and after a cursory wave of our passport.

It was a trip that I'll never forget, as luck continued to be on my side. I was hungover from the after-match Guinness-tasting championships on the Saturday evening, and missed the coach taking the squad back to Bective's clubhouse for a Sunday lunch buffet meal. My roommate had found it hilarious to leave me snoozing, after I'd already got up nice and early, managed to eat a large breakfast, then dropped back to sleep again. Fumbling around the hotel reception area in a panic, I was spotted by some committee members, and without hesitation I was invited to a five-star hotel for a five-course Sunday lunch with them.

After my free a la carte meal, I returned to the clubhouse grinning like a Cheshire cat and thought it only polite to buy some of the committee a drink. But as I collected orders, some of the players had stacked my tab with a dozen pints of Guinness, and the total cost was eye-watering. It was already well documented that a friend and I had been so well looked after by our hosts the previous evening, spending a meagre £4.80, that my teammates thought it right to stitch me up as best they could. The bell had already gone for last orders, when the Chairman of Bective Rangers announced that the bar was now shutting and the last drinks were all on the house. It seemed that my luck was never-ending that weekend.

During pre-season training for the Saints in 1986, I had the freedom to take more time off from the Royal Navy than usual, as I prepared to leave the Services in a few months' time. But it soon became evident that a player who eventually played over 150 games for the Saints was being prioritised over me and another back-row player, for all the wrong reasons. I was assured by my captain and the two coaches that they were voting to get me selected for the first team, but were being outvoted by four committee members, who may have been influenced by family ties with the player in question.

Having sampled the ill effects of favouritism or 'politics' when bobsleighing in 1983, a policy that may have cost me an opportunity to run at a World Cup in Lake Placid and the Sarajevo Winter Olympics, it was very disturbing for me to then hear that selection decisions weren't being viewed on merit at Northampton. To rub salt into the wound, a marine officer, who on occasion I'd kept out of the Navy and Combined Services teams, ridiculed me by saying that I was sixth-choice No.8 in the Midlands, whilst he picked up an England B cap in the same position, for joining the right club at the right time.

Needing a challenge to play at my best, I therefore made it my priority to get to the bottom of whether or not I was in the Saints' first-team plans for the season, so I tracked down the first-team manager. I asked what I needed to do to become a regular choice, hoping for an encouraging chat and wondering if my fitness, ability or attitude was in question. I would have responded positively if this were the case and without question done something about it. To hear his one sentence reply was the final nail in the coffin when he said, "Don't worry; you get paid to come up and see your girlfriend at the weekends, don't you?"

To say that I felt despondent was an understatement as I thought I was playing some of my best rugby, and I was happy to travel from Dorset during midweek, to join in with pre-season training. The coaching staff did their best to make me feel part of the squad, but trying to convince me that I'd make a good modern-day second row player fell on deaf ears, although I played there once or twice to show further commitment. Travel expenses had been cut to a maximum limit of £10 per game, leaving me out of pocket each week, but my enthusiasm and passion for the sport remained second to none. Eventually, enough was enough and along with other first- team players, including another back-rower, I left the Saints. A little while later the club management was restructured, a decision that eventually proved to be very productive for the long-term future of the club, and I was approached by a committee member to see if I'd rejoin them again. I had enjoyed my time at Northampton, making good friends with some players and supporters, but my mind was made up to leave, and I did so after playing my last game against Leicester for the 2nd XV.

Feeling confident that I could challenge for a Midlands place at blindside wing forward, I made a decision to track down a Combined Services player who played at Leicester Tigers, to see if I could join them. However, that same week, Bedford made a bid to recruit me, and it coincided with my friend from Leicester and several other quality forwards moving club to play for the Blues, including a current England international second row. It was a move that over the next five years allowed me the opportunity to be rewarded for my efforts, playing one-hundred-and-fourteen games and winning promotion to Division 1 of the National Leagues (now called The Premiership), being invited to attend training sessions with the Midlands squad, and been given the honour of captaining the team in 1990-91. It was a happy time for me, and a two-week tour to Kenya in 1987 was the icing on the cake. I am eternally grateful to the club for the opportunity to be selected for the 1st XV, purely on merit, and for the welcome and care I received throughout my time there.

My involvement with rugby diminished over the coming years, at a time when my faith blossomed, but I still go and watch the odd live game from time to time. In 2018, I attended an ex-players' reunion at Kettering, a club I played for as a nineteen-year-old, and a couple of friends quickly ushered me next to a player, after he'd professed to attending church. They thought that we'd be better suited to chat to each other, after light-heartedly ridiculing the both of us about our faith. I hadn't previously been aware that he attended church, but he seemed very evangelistic about it and I encouraged him that it was a good thing. I must have appeared shocked to hear the good news, before saying that I didn't realise that he had a faith, in the hope of hearing his testimony and how he served his church, etc. However, his response was disappointing, when he replied, "Of course I've got a f***g faith, most of us have!"

Our walk of faith is a lifetime journey, but I'm convinced that when we draw close to God he is able to work far better with us, and one of the first things that happened when I became a Christian in 1997 was that I stopped swearing immediately. It was as if my tongue had been replaced with an upgraded model, but I quickly recognised it as a real blessing and, together with other behavioural changes, it was not something that I could have engineered. I still attended the odd social event at Kettering to mix with the people I'd known for many years, having played there as a teenager and then coached after retiring from playing. However, after one such social, I let out a crass word and felt so ashamed with myself that I made a decision to restrict my drinking of alcohol thereafter. It was also a time when my identity as 'an ex-first-team coach' was eroding, and rightly so as I hadn't been involved for around a year. The downside was that any perceived status that I still held was slowly being replaced with disrespectful taunts or challenges about my faith, but only from a few of the players.

Two incidents stand out. The first was when a guy who I knew well suddenly appeared and had to be held back, telling me that my children were no better than his, and who was I to think that I was a better father than him! I remained calm and politely told him that I thought nothing of the sort and that we should have a chat on another occasion when he'd calmed down. Why he thought such things or chose to confront me with such venom, I have never asked, and on the rare occasions that we've met since, things have been very amicable.

The second incident involved someone who thought it would be fun to ridicule me in front of a group of players, challenging my credentials as a no nonsense player and coach, now assuming that I'd gone soft for attending church and becoming religious!

I considered it to be one of the toughest things in my life when I chose to follow Christ, as there is a submission and vulnerability in doing so, and to step over the threshold of the entrance doors to my church for the first time was very difficult. This person's assumption that I'd become religious was also way out, a comment that I took to mean I'd become a member of a church and was therefore ritualistic and holier than thou. Instead I'd become a man of faith, confident in the hope (and truth) that scripture proclaimed and assured about things I couldn't see (Hebrews ch.11). My rapid transformation, from the inside out, was testimony to what was happening to me, and something that some people seemed happy to ridicule, whilst others respected. This person was someone I'd known for many years as a businessman and Freemason, so I let him rant on, until his confidence became too out of hand. I then politely asked "Why are you a Freemason if you don't believe in God. Could you tell me which God you believe in, or is it just for extra business and networking that you've joined?" His embarrassment was tangible as he swore, and then turned away, with the group of friends now pushing him around whilst laughing at him.

When Freemasons take their oaths, that I think are spiritually misleading, they are saying that they believe there is one God (or supreme being), accepting that a person can employ many different ways to seek and to express what they know of God as 'The Grand Architect of the Universe'. I wonder if by taking the many oaths that he did, my friend had become more religious than me. Jesus said in John ch.14 v.6,

"I am the way and the truth and the life. No one comes to the Father except through me."

Aged thirty-six years old, I decided that this was a statement I wanted to explore, challenge or accept.

Sensing acceptance and belonging is paramount to feeling comfortable in any surroundings, and I began to feel uncomfortable in the rugby clubhouse for a whole host of reasons, so I left and didn't go back for many years. Similarly, there is a misconception that you need to be a really good person before attending church regularly, when the message should be to welcome anyone with open arms, where love, care and protection is evident and without being judgemental. A person can then make a well-balanced decision about their personal commitment, either at a club or a church, if they first feel welcomed!

There was a time when I felt especially welcomed and accepted when I discovered that my passion was more towards football than any other sport, even though I adopted rugby as my main participation game from the age of eleven. My loyalty towards Sheffield Wednesday was always fragile and based on family tradition, until I was influenced to watch Sheffield United play, when a friend invited me to watch them. Some might say that I was converted from an Owl to a Blade, the clubs' nicknames, when I began regularly attending Sheffield United games, as

14

the sport is viewed like a religion in some circles! I had linked up with Dave at the age of fourteen and felt an instant camaraderie, when he introduced me to his friend Mel, an ex-Merchant Seaman who'd lost an eye fighting at some stage in his life. Mel was in his mid-twenties, part of the Sheffield United hooligan element, called the Shoreham Republican Army (SRA), which was discreet in their tactics, very rarely getting identified, but brutal in their ways.

By the time I was fifteen, I was mixing with a circle of friends that encouraged me to start travelling to some away matches. However, I gradually became aware that I was getting out of my depth the more I pushed my boundaries, terrified, yet excited at what I was witnessing in and around the ground at Bramall Lane. Running battles between opposition supporters were commonplace, but I managed to avoid getting beaten up or having to land a kick or punch, even as the danger was getting closer and closer. Part of the Saturday afternoon fun was to venture down the side streets before and after matches, following a crowd that craved confrontation. The away supporters had to make their way back to the railway station from the ground, a short trip that was less than a mile long, yet the longest journey from safety many away supporters would ever make. By now Dave was leaning more towards Mel's influence, having been well groomed by his mentor, whilst I'd become adept at making excuses to shirk off, eventually deciding to attend home games only, but with less-intimidating mates.

I made many decisions during my early teens that made me realise that I had a gentle character, with a competitive edge, rather than a foolish person with a violent streak. The adventure of being part of the crowd eventually subsided, but only when I watched up to a hundred QPR fans get seriously injured after being trapped in a forecourt. The chaotic scene was hard to watch, as some United hooligans pelted the away fans with anything they could lay their hands on. It was a dreadful and barbaric sight as bodies fell to the ground where they once stood. A policeman began forcefully clearing away spectators and hooligans alike, thumping me on the side of my face after I found myself in the wrong place at the wrong time, and I was in no mood to hang around after that! Instead I sprinted to the nearest bus stop to get home as quickly as possible.

Whilst I loved the thought of being a loyal supporter, I felt disgusted by the way these people had acted, showing no mercy to those they were stoning, almost tribal in their devotion to protecting their misplaced honour. That same season – and a real turning point for me – was when a Sheffield United thug held a Newcastle supporter on the ground, yanking his head up by his hair, beckoning myself and other sideliners to kick him in the head. For some this proved an irresistible offer, but for me it was a sickening incident that was easy to walk away from. Crucially, it was an act that allowed me to make up my mind to turn my back on football hooliganism, and it left me relieved that I'd done so. Unfortunately, my thirst for a buzz still got the better of me only a few months later, when I received a severe beating behind the NAAFI bar, during my time as a young naval recruit!

As my rugby-playing career developed in the Armed Forces, so did my laddish behaviour. I was taken on my first rugby tour, which was over a long weekend in Manchester, when I was still only seventeen and playing at outside centre or wing, whichever position suited the team best. I'd initially declined the offer to tour with the Air Station rugby team at Yeovilton, as I hated all the after-match singing, and the thought of drinking heavily for four days had very little appeal. However, I was given no option but to attend by the senior rates that made up a big part of the squad, as they'd already organised the time off for me.

I knew I was in trouble the moment a nutter of a Physical Training Instructor insisted that I sit next to him, promising that he'd look after me. He already had a can of beer to his lips when I took my seat beside him at 8.30am, with the rest of the beer case tucked under his seat, so it was no surprise when by late morning a squad of giddy sailors took their place in the food queue of a service station. Remaining polite but noisy, we lined up behind each other with our food trays to hand, but by the time we'd all got to the till and paid for just a coffee or a mug of tea, there was a trail of open sandwich cartons, empty plates and discarded food left on the floor behind us. Who said there's no such thing as a free meal! It was even more of a shock to discover the amount of alcohol some of the players were drinking, knowing that we had a game that same afternoon.

The weekend was going well, and my confidence to push limits, knowing that I had people taking responsibility for me, was increasing as I got more boisterous. A challenge was made to obtain the best souvenir, by fair means or foul, to decorate the base's rugby club, a small corrugated-sheet building in the middle of the camp. It was already fancifully decorated with acquired goodies, primarily from other rugby clubs or public houses that had previously been visited, and I made it my mission to find the biggest and best trophy the club had ever seen.

The boot of the fifty-seater coach was only partially full with a mixture of team possessions and attained gifts, when my initial contribution of a line-painting machine, still half-full with white marking paint was declined. We were now on our return trip home when we pulled in at a motorway service station for lunch, and it was then that I spotted my opportunity for stardom. Parked up in a bay, no more than ten metres away from the coach, was a large funfair trailer with a tarpaulin that was covering a yellow children's merry-go-round car. In my drunken haze I managed to get the car half in and half out of the trailer, before I realised how heavy it was, but I was now stuck with a dead weight resting heavily on my forearms. Fortunately, the rest of the team came to my rescue, after they'd spotted me whilst they were crossing over the motorway on a glass bridge that linked the two service stations. The driver was ordered to get going as quickly as possible, but not before the boot was emptied to make room for the fairground vehicle, that proved to be a worthy winner of the souvenir challenge.

After competing for the Fleet Air Arm at Earl's Court in the Royal Tournament Field Gun Competition for a second time in 1981, six of us booked a holiday to Ibiza. This turned out to be quite a holiday for all the mischievous but adventurous reasons, as the whole of San Antonio seemed to want to party, whether it be day or night. What started out as an evening coach trip, where we ate and drank as much as we wanted, suddenly turned into a potential riot. As over two-hundred young adults, who came from the same hotel, took their places, a small contingent seemed to take a dislike to us. Our group was made up from all ages and various hotels, which had been signed up on an independent outing and placed closest to them.

It may have been the copious amounts of Sangria taking effect on me, after managing to obtain and hide several jugs under the table, or a macho reaction to some of our party winding me up! Whatever the reason, I took it upon myself to make good use of the leftover baked potatoes and chopped-up bread, creating a humdinger of a food fight, after the other tables began shouting obscenities and football chants towards us.

Things came to a sudden halt at the right time, as insults continued to escalate between the tables and after staff and reps failed to quell the bad feeling. But I've never sobered up so fast as when I looked down from the solid wooden table, that I was now standing on, to see an officer of the Civil Guard unclip his holster then point his pistol at me. My five friends and I calmed down instantly, and I was pleased to get back on the coach in one piece some time later.

On this same holiday our group of six decided it would be good to go and see a bullfight at a nearby bullring. Basking in the sunshine with our takeaway burgers and bottles of lager, made for a perfect evening of relaxation, but as the night wore on we all began to feel a little bit heartless at what we were eating and what we'd signed up for. The atrocity of what was happening to the animals caught me out, and as the quality and skill levels of the matador built up, so did the size of the bull and the cheering and baying for blood from the crowd. We eventually walked out disturbed by what we'd seen and heard, but not quite understanding how this could be considered a happy and regular family outing for the locals!

The bulls are selected and condemned to a brutal death from birth and appear emaciated when they enter the ring. The animal is then taunted by several officials to weaken and frustrate it, before being tortured with small spears to the neck that allows bloodletting and further weakening as it gallops around chasing after the antagonists. After a while the matador assumes all authority and power over the animal before it is innocently slaughtered, to the cheers of the crowd! Little did I know that sixteen years later, someone that I learnt to adore had already suffered similar condemnation, torture, taunts and humiliation, before being brutally murdered around two thousand years before.

A posting to Royal Naval Air Station Portland followed my holiday abroad but my hedonistic lifestyle continued, fuelled by heavy drinking and sometimes four or five nights a week. Although the summer season was one long party, New Year's Eve in Weymouth was hard to beat. I'd been collected from Bath Rugby Club, after playing rugby in the afternoon, pre-arranged before going home to Sheffield on leave a couple of weeks earlier. Charlie Chaplin is best remembered for his comedic, silent movies of the 1920s and 30s, which were still being regularly shown on TV throughout my childhood and beyond. It was a great surprise, then, to see that a friend of mine had taken immense effort to dress up exactly like Charlie for the annual New Year's Eve fancy dress festivities.

My outfit consisted of a one-piece fluorescent green and yellow acrylic garment that had previously served as part of my bobsleigh suit. Other mix-and-match kit included a diver's face mask, snorkel and a whopping great pair of professional scuba diver's flippers that were a nightmare to walk in. The town centre was heaving and you were definitely in the minority if you weren't wearing fancy dress. A group of eight or nine of us were now in full flow on a pub crawl, when I spotted three gents wearing normal clothing and trying to act cool. The clattering sound of my fins hitting the ground was already creating hysteria wherever we went, when I decided to push limits a little further and used my snorkel as a straw. I carefully bent the piece of plastic over one of the cool guy's shoulder, straight into his pint glass and sucked up most of his drink, then quickly pointed it upwards whist blowing out as hard as possible!

The low-level ceiling dispersed what seemed to be gallons of fluid into the immediate surroundings, but mainly into the rim of my friend's bowler hat and the three gents' hair. Charlie Chaplin had been drowned and his make-up, now streaking down his face, made him look like something out of a horror movie. Before the cool guys had a chance to get too annoyed about their hair being wet, I was patting them on their back and wishing them a Happy New Year as we dispersed in hysterics. The fins stomped down like the beat to bongo drums as we made our way to the pub exit, with Charlie following but not knowing whether to laugh or cry, as his pristine outfit dripped wet with beer.

Many years later a friend and I went to watch Bedford play Bristol in the semi-final, first leg of the Championship play-offs, almost twenty-five years to the day when I retired from playing there. I bumped into an ex- coach, Richard, the man that guided us to promotion to Division 1 (now called the Premiership) of the national leagues in 1989, who reminded me of an incident that same year when we played Coventry, at our home ground in Goldington Road. I was playing at No.8, following the ball out to the wing, when the supporters in the main stand erupted into loud jeers, right in front of me. Turning around, I saw that the six front-row players were having a bit of a disagreement with each other some fifty metres away, resulting in punches being thrown. As the fighting escalated, I decided that I needed to do something about it, so began my testosterone-fuelled sprint back towards the melee, targeting a second-row player who I'd had some previous history with. As I came within distance, I drop-kicked him, which knocked him over and left several bodies strewn all around us like skittles in a ten-pin bowling game.

Some of the players were oblivious to my antics, unable to understand how the fight had suddenly ended, yet others looked in amazement and were left totally bewildered with my actions. Fortunately, for me and the reputation of the club, the referee had missed the incident, eventually sending off a prop from each team. As it turned out and probably due to my poor eyesight, I'd inadvertently targeted the other opposition second row, who I knew to be a Royal Air Force player and not someone I thought ill of. My pride wouldn't allow me to apologise for hitting the wrong guy, in fact quite the opposite, but deep down I felt sorry for him and there was no lasting damage. It was more a sense of fulfilling my duty for the team, justified by aiming for someone that had tried injuring me in previous games, albeit a serious error of judgement on my part.

Richard commented that it reminded him that our country was always in safe hands knowing that when called upon, our servicemen could be relied on to sort things out by always leading from the front. We both agreed that what I did would have resulted in a long, if not a lifetime ban from playing the sport, if it happened today. The match was being televised by Anglia, and when the edited highlights were shown on the evening news the report suggested that this was the darker side of Rugby Union.

That same year I was invited to attend a couple of Midlands' squad training sessions at Moseley Rugby Club, and I realised then that I could have easily blown the opportunity to play at this higher representative level, if the selectors had got to hear about my ill-discipline. As it was, a disastrous game against Llanelli, when the Midlands selectors arrived secretly to watch me, sealed my fate for any future consideration of representing the region. I was left feeling disheartened, particularly as we had several changes in the pack and my usual scrum-half had been rested, factors that allowed the Welsh forwards to push us around and keep us on the back foot for most of the game. I didn't help my case when my frustration boiled over after we were penalised at a scrum and I picked up the ball in one hand, slamming it into the ground aggressively. Expressing my frustration in this way was totally out of character, and my petulant reaction proved costly, ending any further dreams of playing at a higher level.

There seemed to be an unwritten law, primarily at coaching level, that those who had a reputation to take matters into their own hands were often coveted. However, committee members would tread cautiously with their views at an official level, but were often found supporting the same principles as their coaches in private surroundings. That the reputation of the club was always of more importance than any individual player was a view that I fully endorsed, but trying to play hard and within the laws of the game was getting more difficult during the late-1980s.

Merit tables were gradually introduced, where promotion and relegation began to affect the traditional standing of the top clubs. As a senior club you were almost guaranteed retaining your top-flight fixtures, no matter what sort of season you'd had previously. The changes meant that there was added pressure to perform at a high intensity week after week and where winning meant everything. It was well known, but rarely challenged, that some teams were attracting new players with cash payments and perks. One of the more amusing careers changes that I heard about was when a top international was lured away from his farming heritage to become a London stockbroker, virtually overnight. On a personal note, when I turned up for my first training session at Bedford, I was asked by two teammates, who themselves were new recruits to the club, why I hadn't got a brand new BMW like theirs. I felt only slightly envious, and far more pleased to be given a chance to gain a first-team place and feel settled at a club, rather than being attracted by perks.

As my responsibilities became greater so my frustration and desire to win could sometimes boil over, particularly when I was appointed captain of the 1st XV. My mandate was to keep the team from sliding straight into league three during the 1990-91 season, after suffering relegation from National League One to Two previously. I knew this was going to be my last year playing the game that I loved, and I was only thirty years old, but the odds seemed stacked against me. I'd only managed to play nine games as vice-captain in our relegation season, due to a series of injuries to my neck and shoulders, and we lost sixteen senior players to retirement or by moving onto other clubs, making the first team's average age just twenty-four. We were tipped for back-to-back relegations, but when interviewed by Anglia, such was my confidence that I resolutely stated that we wouldn't be relegated at any cost, because I wouldn't allow it to happen. Looking back, it was a rash statement to make but my instinct and boldness proved correct, mainly because a short while later the club managed to recruit two well-seasoned forwards from Gloucester.

I regularly played against adults from the age of sixteen, at outside centre or winger, for my Air Station team on Wednesday afternoons. By the age of nineteen, I'd moved in to the back row, and two years later I'd become a first-choice regular for the Royal Navy team, whilst playing for US Portsmouth at weekends and Hampshire during the County Championship competition. The one-hundred-and-seventy-four-mile round trip from Portland to Portsmouth proved my ambition to progress in the sport, but like all the teams I played for, until my last two seasons at Bedford, I don't feel I ever received one-to-one coaching of any consequence.

From the age of seventeen I'd bulked up considerably, after carrying out eight months' intensive training during my first stint representing the Fleet Air Arm Field Gun Crew. For a majority of the rugby season I was still being released from duty at weekends, to play representative rugby for the Royal Navy and Combined Services Colts as a winger, and weighing in at around fourteen-and-a-half stone. Carrying light muscle strains or sprains was the norm, and rugby laws stated that no protective padding was allowed to be worn. However, sticky plaster, tape or bandages were deemed appropriate, so long as it was covering an injury, but it wasn't something you really wanted to advertise to the opposition.

As a forward, my weight had increased to over sixteen stone, but debilitating injuries were becoming more common, and during a game for the Royal Navy against the Civil Service, the wrist to my right hand buckled under and touched the underside of my right forearm. The area was x-rayed and although no breaks or cracks were obvious, the injury was treated as being a fractured scaphoid bone, one of the smallest bones in the body. Six weeks later the plaster cast was removed, but I never recovered full flexibility or strength in my wrist again. Afterwards, it was suggested that I taped a thin aluminium strip down my forearm, into the palm, so that it held my weakened wrist joint at a 45-degree angle. As one of my weapons of choice was a mighty hand-off, I needed to radically adapt my game. I therefore ensured that the rounded edges of the aluminium were always well-covered with padding and sticky tape, confident that no damage would ever be inflicted to another player by the support.

The Royal Navy selectors were happy to see me back playing a few weeks later, and I was never questioned about the bandaging by any player or official right up to the end of my playing career in 1991. I'd generally adapted well to using my hips and shoulder when making contact, but occasionally impulse got the better of me, resulting in full frontal contact with my forearm, as compensation for my now debunked hand-off. Naturally, this didn't always go down too well with the opposition, leading to altercations from time to time, but I wasn't a nasty player and there was never any intent to seriously harm anyone. To see cowardliness played out so violently on a rugby park, where the brutality of the offence caused serious damage, was unusual, and I can only wonder what sort of person would do such a thing to an undefended player! Playing for Northampton against Harlequins, I saw our scrum-half have his jaw broken as he ran through the defence after chipping the ball ahead, and our scrum-half at Bedford suffered the same injury after being taken out by a thundering punch from behind whilst playing against Coventry. Both incidents made me reflect on how vulnerable we all were when playing the game, and a person decides to overstep the line of disciplined aggression into undisciplined and blatant thuggery.

One of my first games for the Royal Navy was against Bristol, under floodlights, at the Memorial Ground in front of a hostile crowd. They had several international players in their ranks, all keen to put us in our place, particularly focussing on one of our props as he'd been approached to play for Bath, their local rivals. The game was developing into a nasty affair, when I packed down at a scrum whilst playing at blindside wing forward. The scrum collapsed but the Bristol front row remained upright, a clear sign that they'd purposely slipped their binding. The tactic left me face down in the muddy ground, pointing inwards, adjacent to our prop's taped head, when suddenly, without warning a boot slammed down on to his exposed cheek. The ferocity of the stamp was meant to damage him and he let out a sickening, high-pitched squeal that intimated they'd succeeded in doing so. Instantly, a large, bloody gash appeared on his cheek, making me feel anxious and somewhat nervous as I stood up and moved away from the scene.

A few minutes later I was pleased to see him regain his composure, after it was determined that the injury was only a deep graze, rather than having split open the skin. Things settled down afterwards, even though the referee took an easy option and indicated that he'd missed the foul play, asking the front-row players to be careful where they put their feet from now on. Having had a healthy respect for the Bristol pack prior to the game, I was left feeling let down by their inappropriate behaviour, before asking myself whether or not I wanted to continue playing at this level, with this sort of antagonism and potential for injury. My answer was a resounding 'yes', but with an attitude that no player was ever going to get the better of me from now on, and with Nan's influential but unwise words ringing in my ears from many years earlier- 'to never back down in a fight.'

Although I maintain that I was never a nasty player, some of my experiences allowed me to sense when a game needed a greater or lesser level of commitment, and I am forever grateful that I avoided playing against a particular New Zealand All Black for a second time, after his team were on tour and I played against him for the Royal Navy. I'd been warned by a Northampton teammate, who was a Royal Air Force player, that I and other potential Combined Services players would be targeted for being 'taken out.' This was something that had been witnessed previously, during their other tour games against the Army and Royal Air Force, but it was the first time that I'd ever heard of such a policy. Their final game was to be against the British Combined Services, so they seemed to be systematically injuring players that were due to play in this fixture, as a way to weaken the team.

Matchday arrived, and from the outset it was intensely physical, with the referee struggling to maintain control. After just twenty minutes one of the best players in the world decided to take me out with a thundering hook to my temple, as I ran at the opposition from a quickly tapped penalty. So discrete was he that very few people saw the incident, but those that did were shocked by the callous act. I played rugby knowing that a bad injury could finish not only my playing career but also my working career, and what he did was beyond the limits of playing hard. I viewed it as outright cowardice.

I was concussed for over twenty-five minutes, oblivious to the fact as I played on for several of those minutes, before being taken off, and then admitted to hospital for overnight monitoring. The incident took me a full week to adequately recover from, but I didn't realise how deeply the psychological effect had on me as it lay dormant for many years. I vowed vengeance for the cynical action if I ever played against him again, convincing myself that I'd break his jaw. Fortunately, I've since learnt that bitterness breeds hatred, something that I never want to experience again. To crave retribution meant that I remained the victim, until I was able to forgive him, something I was able to do, but only when I converted to Christianity many years later.

I had opportunities to confront the player in question about his actions on two further occasions, when he left New Zealand to play his rugby for a rival club in the Midlands. He was asked to take a coaching session whilst I played at Bedford and later when I coached at Kettering, but my resentment of the man was still so deeply ingrained within me, that I made excuses not to attend the sessions. Did I hate the man enough to break his jaw, as I'd pledged? I doubt it, as I've never hit an undefended man with any ferocity and I couldn't have lived with myself for doing so. Thankfully, I now have a peace about the incident and bear no malice, after genuinely having forgiven him.

During a four-team tournament in Sicily during the close season, I found myself targeted for rough treatment during one of the games against a Welsh club. The team I represented was called 'El Presidente Invitation XV' and was made up of a group of players who'd been invited over by an Italian hairdresser, who had links with Bedford. The squad was made up from several clubs and not all from senior teams or even first-fifteen regulars for that matter, something that left us at a great disadvantage. It was amusing to be met at the airport by our flamboyant president and some bodyguards, which left us wondering why a dentist should need guarding! I can only guess that there were mafia connections, but he managed to get us through customs without any queuing, so we were very grateful for that. A handful of us were hosted at the same hotel as Bridgend, who came over with a first-team squad that had Welsh international representatives, unlike ourselves who didn't even have a coach and who'd volunteered for a free 'jolly'.

The Welsh boys had no intention of talking to any of us, doing their best to psyche us out as we sunbathed around the pool or ate together in the restaurant, which seemed absurd and over the top. On the evening of the game I was made captain of a bunch of mainly non-English speaking Italians, several of whom I'd only just met an hour before kick-off. Naturally, we were being overrun at times, but we defended well and created some cohesive moves, particularly from the back row where I played, together with another Bedford teammate.

Unfortunately, as I was directing a defensive line from a maul, a Welsh second-row player decided to run into my pointed finger whilst in full flow. The incident floored the guy but it was clear that my words weren't being accepted as an apology, so my ego kicked in and I told him what I really thought of him. Naturally, he wanted to rip my head off, for what he convinced himself was a deliberate act of violence, and the whole of the Bridgend pack made it clear what they thought of me some moments later, when I was caught on the floor a couple of times.

The overzealous rucking was enough for the selectors to take me off as a precautionary measure, but our other games against Treviso and Toulouse were much friendlier affairs, with the French club turning it on against Bridgend in the final match to win the tournament.

On tour in Nairobi, Kenya, during Bedford's centenary season in 1987, we found ourselves playing a fixture against Mwamba, a university old boys' team. The referee had come out of retirement to officiate the match and was making blatantly biased decisions against us from the kick-off. We'd previously had warnings from our organisers about how poor the referee might be, but this was verging on diabolical. To compensate for my frustrations, I decided to show a more physical, rumbustious side to my play, with my impatience eventually getting the better of me as I began stamping on several players that were lying offside. I received a verbal warning by the official, and our captain was told that any other violent incidents would result in a player being sent off. I managed to curtail my aggression at a time when more of our players began to lose their cool, in response to the persistent, cheating antics of the ref.

In a flash, a full-scale brawl erupted after a scrum and I instantly turned away so as not to get involved, knowing that I would likely be targeted by the official for an early bath. Incredibly, I was attacked from behind by my opposite number, who knocked me to the floor, before I was beaten and kicked by several of the opposition, whilst curled up on the ground. As the fighting calmed down, I, together with their No.8 was sent off, although I must have been the only player not to have landed a punch. So much for never backing down in a fight! My shirt had been torn and ripped off my back after the battering, so I walked off to the pitchside bench showing a bare chest, which may have further provoked the jeering crowd.

To my sheer horror, the rickety, wooden stand bounced up and down as several hundred young men, most with bottles of beer in their hands, slammed their feet down in unison, pointing at me as they sang an unnerving, tribal chant. The expectation of some glass bottles being hurled at us was real, and I found it difficult to sit with my back to the crowd for a few minutes. The tension and cold chill to my spine only subsided when play resumed and after the crowd had settled again. I felt really hard done by after this event, as the emergency disciplinary panel voted that I miss the next game of the tour against the Kenyan national team, and it was to be the first and only time that I was sent off.

However, the tables were turned when I played at Roundhay for the Royal Navy, under floodlights in dense fog some years earlier. Regular outbursts of fighting were breaking out around the field, and the whole experience wasn't particularly pleasant. Nevertheless, it has been a cause for some amusement over the years, as my friend recently reminded me, and some compensation, if you could call it that, for my sending-off in Kenya. Visibility was down to around twenty metres when a fight broke out, the referee deciding to send off my teammate Scooby, a second-row juggernaut and more of a peacemaker than most. As he argued his case, insisting that it wasn't him who'd landed 'the punch', the referee was dismissive of his pleas and insisted that he leave the field straight away. I could see that he was upset and frustrated by the injustice of the decision, desperate to name me as the perpetrator, and rightly so.

With traditional naval humour, a teammate and I began verbally supporting the ref, flippantly waving our hands at our own player in disgust, before pointing our fingers for Scooby to leave the field. His face was a picture as I hid behind the referee's back, struggling to contain my laughter. It was to be the one and only time that he was sent off during his playing career, and we still remain good friends to this day. Unfortunately, Scooby's rugby career was cut short when he was blinded in one eye, after a ball hit him whilst playing hockey. He'd just left the Navy and was completing his basic training to start a new career in the Cambridgeshire police force when the incident happened, and after confirming that he would join Kettering, where I was coaching at the time. Neither his police career or his rugby ambitions were fulfilled after this unfortunate accident, and I admire his ongoing resilience after such a dreadful misfortune.

Some years earlier, Scooby and myself were selected to tour with the Naval Air Command to Berlin, when we were billeted at Army barracks adjacent to Spandau Prison, a place where Rudolph Hess (one of Hitler's right-hand men) was once the sole inmate interned there. As we settled in, I'd spotted the locker where a couple of the players had hidden a cooked rump of beef, diligently acquired from the camp kitchens the day before when the chefs weren't looking. During our night out on the town, I had a discussion with Scooby about getting back early before the rest of the team, raiding the locker and scoffing the joint between the two of us. The mention of food was too much of a temptation to bear for either of us, so we left abruptly, forgetting that the third-floor sleeping quarters had previously been locked up when we departed to play a game that afternoon.

My disappointment at being confronted with a locked door was short-lived, when I discovered that one of the dormer windows that protruded from the rooftop had been left open. I quickly climbed through the landing window, on to the slates, with a unique view down in to the floodlit courtyard of Spandau Prison, which the Russians were guarding. The heavy rain didn't deter my enthusiasm to acquire my free meal, speedily scampering along to the nearby window, without much thought about slipping. But the toxic cocktail of alcohol, adrenalin and foolishness had kicked in when my terrified, eighteen-stone friend ventured onto the rooftop.

The idea to begin throwing apples at Scooby came from a bowl of fruit left nearby, forcing him to hug the slippery tiles with all his might as he cursed and swore at me from his prostrate position. After my calls for prison inmate Rudy, to sleep well, and then assuring my mate that there would be no more missiles launched towards him, I was able to drag him through the window of the dormitory to safety. He survived the ordeal and we managed to force open the locker and enjoy our high-protein meal, kindly leaving a tiny morsel of beef for the rest of the team to enjoy.

During the tour we were allowed to play on pitches adjacent to the site of the original stadium where Hitler had attended the 1936 Olympic Games. Although we beat no sporting world records on the pitch, drinking steins of lager with bottles of wine chasers must have been a first, and worthy of an entry into the Guinness Book of Records. Our squad of players ventured into the city centre, already worse for wear, setting up camp in the main Bierkeller, which slowly filled to capacity as the evening wore on. The ageing band members were already set up and playing on a central stage when we arrived, kitted out in full Bavarian attire, when it became time for them to have a break.

Like a magpie, I was instantly attracted to the shining silver trumpet left on stage, knowingly looking over at a friend whose intentions were similar to mine. Within seconds a non-harmonious din filled the venue, from our attempt at playing the trumpet and drums together, trying to coax more of the team on stage as we did so. But before I'd warmed the instrument up, I found myself being attacked by members of the band, the trumpet player taking several potshots at me before I realised what was happening. There seemed to be a real hatred towards us as we were virtually kicked off stage, before deciding that it was best to leave the venue after the band refused to carry on playing.

I hope that I will be remembered for being an honest (except for the Roundhay game), reliable rugby player who could adapt to the importance of the occasion. I rarely went too far, but a large part of my game involved heavy, full contact, which was used as a statement of intent when the need arose. Rugby is still a highly physical game, although there is far more protection from foul play now, particularly after a change of law allowing officials to intervene in support of the referee. I was taught to exploit weaknesses, and encouraged, from a young age, to use my physical presence in contact situations. Words like intimidate, dominate or retribution were often used by coaches to imply that the forwards should take control of a game when appropriate, and I would argue that I knew no different by my mid-twenties. I had a frustrating end to my playing career, retiring prematurely after the damage to my neck and other recurring injuries began to take their toll.

How ironic that a local derby game against Northampton Saints was the point of no return, as far as the damage to my neck was concerned. Hitting a ruck with poor technique as full-time approached aggravated previous damage in my neck, and left me wondering if I'd broken it. A numb sensation and a loss of strength left me with a sense that my head was dangling on a piece of elastic, and it was an injury that led to me missing more games than I played during my last two seasons. Twenty-three years later, and after recurring nerve and muscular pain, it was identified that I have stenosis and spondylosis to C5 and C6 discs. The damage has left me with symptoms similar to whiplash, which have compressed and misaligned the two discs.

In becoming a Christian, I had reason to wrestle with the idea about whether or not I could have played rugby at the level I achieved, with the attitude I had towards my opponents. I now know that I would have to have adapted my game, which may or may not have made me a better player. As a Christian All Black advised me some years later, after questioning him about how he deals with the dilemma of foul play, "If you get hit, you don't retaliate but your next tackle is the hardest one you'll ever make." Another Christian friend summed it up when he said, "If you play outside of the rules of any sport, you're cheating. If you cheat, you have to question how good a player you really are."

A new phenomenon was being discussed in the early 1980s called road rage. I'd previously had reason to curse or swear at drivers, but never felt remotely aggrieved enough to want to chase someone down and confront them. However, it seemed that a lot of people were becoming braver behind the steering wheel of a car and happy for a confrontation.

Just before retiring from playing rugby I was driving home through a quiet village when I found myself daydreaming, and I missed a temporary set of traffic lights that were on red. Realising my mistake, I began reversing, and then noticed a driver who was coming through from the other direction pulling over on the pavement adjacent to me. The man seemed furious and made it clear how upset he was that I'd tried to get through a single lane, whilst the lights were on red. Staring at me, he then began verbalising what he was going to do about it. Unfortunately, he'd triggered something inside of me and before his door was fully open, I was stood over him threatening that if he unclipped his seatbelt, he'd be decked (polite version of events). He was clearly someone who wasn't used to backing down or being challenged in this way, but fortunately he sat tight, allowing me the time to calm down. The on-site road workers kept their head down, avoiding the embarrassment of eye contact with either party as we eventually drove off in opposite directions.

After retiring as a player, I became concerned that I was storing up aggression with no natural outlet to vent any surplus energy. Fortunately, an offer to coach the 1st XV forwards at Kettering proved to be a great option, allowing me to use some of the competitive, abrasive edge that I still retained to give something back to the game. It was a way of gradually stepping back from my twenty-year playing career in a disciplined and controlled environment, rather than having to deal with the frustrations and consequences of an abrupt end. I am most appreciative of how the other first-team coach, Doug, and the chairman, Bill, allowed me the freedom to grow into the position of forwards' coach during this time.

Having a young family was perhaps starting to soften me up, in more ways than I'd realised. During a short trip into the town centre with Natasha, my three-year-old daughter, I became acutely aware of the demise in courteous behaviour when two young teenagers used such an array of foul language, that it stopped me dead in my tracks. So incensed was I at their lack of respect for other people, that I told them so. Needless to say, the young girls looked at me as though I was from another planet, further infuriating me as I walked off shaking my head.

Even now, I always open or hold doors open for others, but I've realised that fewer people seem inclined to acknowledge the polite gesture by saying 'thank you'. I mentioned these incidents to a mate, explaining how I thought society seemed to be changing for the worse, and that 'please' and 'thank you' had all but disappeared from people's mindsets. His response was simple: "Being polite is seen as a sign of weakness, Glyn, that's why".

I was shocked to realise that people's moral compass had become so blurred, enough to be considered a weak person, simply for showing respect to others. Had my values really become so outdated? I'm not trying to say that I was a perfect gentleman, that I never swore or made mistakes, but I'd always managed to be courteous and refrain from swearing whenever women, children or elderly people were around. It seems that words like 'shame', 'ashamed' or 'shameful' have all but disappeared from people's minds, and good morals replaced with a determination to be selfish, thinking only of ourselves no matter who we upset or at what expense to others.

After three years as a coach at Kettering, I stepped down, taking time to concentrate more on running my business and a short while later I began investigating the Christian faith, something that helped me understand far more about myself than I could ever imagine. The things I'd looked upon as a weakness now became a strength and vice versa. Where pride or ego was once a trait, humility began to creep in, and instead of fearing the consequences of an argument, I learnt to discuss and listen to both sides of a story, rather than making assumptions or being judgmental. Furthermore, as my old, ingrained nature continued to dissolve, I sensed gentleness, kindness and patience becoming more prominent in my behaviour.

Knowing that my character was beginning to soften took a time to come to terms with, and some bad habits still resurface and tempt me to this day. But, through ongoing and constant prayer, I trust that my selfishness is being replaced with thoughtfulness, and the burden of striving to achieve has been replaced with an understanding that it's okay to enjoy a challenge and have projects, but equally so to find time to have peace, quiet, and to draw close to God.

A business associate seemed astounded to hear that, as a businessman and an ex-rugby player, I'd become a Christian. As we continued chatting over a coffee, he mentioned about a previous boss of his who'd professed to be a Christian, but who was the biggest hypocrite he'd ever met. He went on to explain how 'pious' and 'religious' this man was on Sundays when he went to church, but that his attitude during the week was as bad as anyone he knew. It prompted me to reply by saying, "I began attending church because I realised that I was imperfect, not perfect, and too many people think you have to be a fully committed Christian to step into church."

I explained that attending church is just a step forward, on what should be a journey of investigation into the faith, a welcoming place where questions can be asked and biblical truths explained. My friend's eyes lit up and he thanked me for saying what I did, before announcing that he'd been auditing our work at sporadic intervals for accounting purposes, and I was relieved to hear that we were his most trusted building contractor. To me, it matters what I do, whether I'm seen or unseen and as a way of fulfilling a lifestyle governed by my love of Jesus Christ. Therefore, my friend's announcement justified my expectations of myself and the way I wanted the business to be run.

If there's anything that sums up my predicament about being a saint or a sinner, it's an incident that occurred when I was working on the doors as a bouncer at a large venue near Weymouth, late one evening. I was in the lobby area when a young woman came in from outside, distressed and screaming that her partner had collapsed and had stopped breathing. I rushed out immediately, to be met by a large group of people that had gathered around him and a guy that I knew, supervising the crowd to stand back and give him space. Without hesitation I checked the man's airways, then gave mouth-to-mouth resuscitation, whilst his girlfriend became more and more hysterical. Within a few moments the patient let out a gasp, before slowly coming around, and I returned back to do my job on the doors.

I was in the right place at the right time, doing a service that was potentially messy, but that many others should have reacted to before me. His girlfriend returned the following week to say thank you, and this time she was much calmer, but initially she didn't identify which one of us had helped out, such was her distress. It transpired that the guy was a sailor who'd had very little to drink but had a seizure or fit of some kind, and as far as he and his girlfriend was concerned, I'd saved his life.

My dilemma is this. On that evening, to some I was a saint (or perhaps a Good Samaritan), as without hesitation I jumped in to help a person I didn't know. I didn't judge and I showed compassion, kindness and there was modesty in not wanting recognition or praise for what I did. To others, I was a sinner, as I'd disobeyed naval protocol by working elsewhere without permission, in a job that was dangerous and with a high risk of injury, and therefore potentially jeopardising my naval career. I was also being paid cash in hand, therefore avoiding the need to pay tax. I can think of several ungodly characteristics that derived from this one incident, such as; defiance and rebellion in avoiding naval protocol, being deceptive and lying when questioned about my work there, and breaking the law by stealing tax money from the government. I would even question whether my modesty was a disguise for the pride I really felt for helping the young man, as I remember being more concerned about any publicity getting back to the naval authorities and getting me in trouble.

Some may say that I wasn't hurting anyone, so what's the problem? I would argue that there are far-reaching consequences to any actions, whether good or bad, and it seems to me that the more we get away with, the more we try to get away with, creating less and less of a conscience within us. God always wanted mankind to live a life that was free from sin, as we can read in Genesis, but after mankind's rebellion he sent Jesus Christ, as fully man, to become a guilt offering, a once-and-for-all sacrificial payment for you and me! God's character is one of perfection, beauty and love and I found it easy to rebel against such things, until I discovered a freedom to live life to the full, as God would want me to, rather than being enslaved to my old ingrained ways. The sacrificial offering that Jesus made suddenly becomes a beautiful, free gift, based on reconciliation with the Father, something that we can't achieve by ourselves, but something that can be obtained by accepting God's grace (undeserved love or favour), by believing and accepting Jesus Christ as our Saviour.

I'm not immune to pressure, illness or temptation, and even as my faith matured, the rigours of running a small but expanding building company, and ensuring that my family came first was often stressful. I remember a time when a tradesman rang the office to tell me about a problem on a job and I let out a minor swear word over the phone, something that caught me out, but not as much as it affected him. Within moments a manager had rung me, alerted by the tradesman that 'Glyn was really upset.' The supervisor asked if I was alright and if he could help in any way, clearly concerned about how annoyed I must have been about something. It was the first time that my staff had heard me swear, and this incident made me realise not only how much I'd changed over the last eight years, but the enormous responsibility on me after professing to follow Jesus' teaching.

Some of these incidents may seem trivial to some of you, but in God's eyes, sin is sin – big, small, malicious, or just a bad thought about something or somebody. I've fallen short on many occasions and scripture tells us that we are to be 'ambassadors for Christ,' set apart and different, which can only be accomplished through the guidance of the Holy Spirit. I'm not better than anybody else, but I want to be a better version of what I was and that still remains the case today.

God knows that we will never be perfect, something I thought I had to be to become a Christian, and just like a good parent wouldn't want us to feel burdened by having to be the best at everything, so God doesn't expect you or I to earn our place in heaven purely by good works and deeds. Whenever I slip up, I know that Jesus has already paid the price for my sins, I am no longer condemned, and that I remain forever forgiven when I'm genuinely sorry for my actions. The Holy Spirit allows me the freedom to fulfil my calling to serve God as he would want me to, by a conviction in my heart to do what is right, and there is both a peace and purpose in that.

I therefore declare myself both Saint and Sinner; but what about you?

In a headlock, 1983, Royal Navy v Army, Twickenham

In support of the ball carrier, Royal Navy v RAF, Twickenham, 1983

Playing for Norhampton Saints v London Welsh, 1984

Combined Services squad v Canada at Portsmouth, 1983
Glyn, back row, 4th from right

Team photo of Bedford Blues whilst captain, 1991

Royal Navy v New Zealand Combined Services; a game which left me severely concussed

Nairobi racecourse, Kenya, with our tour captain and former England captain John Orwin, 1987

Captaining Bedford in one of my last games, 1991

Chapter Two

WHEN I WAS A LAD

The phrase, 'When I was a lad', takes me back to my childhood. It was a time when I encountered lots of fun, some moments of fear, and when I learnt to respect authority, and to stand up for myself. My earliest memory was standing up in a cot, whilst still a toddler, then I can't recall much else until a few years later, when I was taken on my first great adventure.

It was a glorious summer's day, I didn't have a care in the world and I was just a few hundred yards from home after returning from my first trek in to the unknown. However, my dream-like state was soon interrupted when my mum, Pam, began yelling at me from the bottom of the road as I confidently led a group of boys down from the working quarry. The immense cavity formed a backdrop to the perimeter edge of our Sheffield council estate and for many years thereafter.

"Get here now and where do you think you've been!" She was angry, upset, and this was not her normal manner or temperament that was being displayed. "We've been worried sick and the neighbours are out looking for you," she yelled, as she ran towards me crying. Nevertheless, I still received a smacked bottom, more commonly known as a 'good hiding,' as Mum's frustrations and anxiety boiled over. The year was 1964 and I was just four years old.

When my mum was alive, she often chuckled when reminding me about this incident, going on to describe in more detail about my triumphant home coming from a play park, some distance away, back to our house in the district of Shirecliffe in Sheffield. Some of the local residents had been frantically searching for me for some time, their fears unfounded as it turned out, when I'd linked up with a bunch of older boys without notifying anyone, who'd innocently taken me off to play with them. On our return I'd somehow become leader of the pack, full of swagger, as I earnestly marched the group back from my first great adventure. Neither ourselves, or any of our neighbours, had telephones or motor transport, so Mum was beside herself with worry. In addition, she had no way of letting Dad know that I'd been missing until he returned home from work later that evening.

Throughout my life I've had several leadership roles, sometimes enforced on me rather than choosing them, but for many years I lacked confidence in my own ability, constantly avoiding the responsibilities normally associated with being a leader. My limited ambition for promotion whilst serving in the Royal Navy is a case in point, finishing my eleven-year career as an Acting Leading Hand, something my colleagues were achieving within two years of service, albeit most were nearer the age of eighteen rather than sixteen when they joined up. However, I didn't lack passion or ambition in other areas, such as sport or testing out my entrepreneurial skills, both of which seemed to be an ingrained part of my character.

Having been born into working-class surroundings on the Springvale Road council estate before moving to Shirecliffe, prospects and expectations were low, but community spirit abounded. I only have one pictorial record as a reminder of my time living on these council estates, that being a black and white photograph cuddling my newly born sister, Julie. "Keep smiling and hold her tight, or you'll drop her," Mum kept saying.

I was sitting on the settee, trying to retain a glowing smile, whilst we had our photograph taken by a well-dressed man, as the little bundle of fun that I was cradling gradually became more agitated, creating a high degree of discomfort for me as she wriggled on my lap. When I look at the crumpled picture it accentuates the dimples to my smiley face, a sign of a proud brother holding firmly on to my beautiful sister. My dad, Keith, had previously taken me to visit Mum and Julie at Jessop's Hospital, prior to them being allowed home. It was an exciting time as layers of cloth were gently peeled away to reveal my sister's hidden face, on 16th December 1964. I eagerly awaited Dad to produce our 'welcome to this world' gift, comprising of several cream-filled chocolate teddies, which Mum and I finished off without feeling too guilty.

Before starting Reception class, I was given clear instructions to remain at the main gate until Mum came to collect me. My willingness to conform was tested during my first week, when I found myself standing alone after all of the pupils had gone home. The teachers were nowhere to be seen, the playground now empty, but there was still an ice cream van parked up some yards away from the main entrance. When Mum eventually appeared, her concern for my welfare was evident as she began to apologise, then hug me profusely, and it was a pleasant surprise when the kind street vendor approached us with a free ice cream cone, as a reward for being such a good boy and not wandering off. He was concerned that I'd been left by myself, and Mum was more relieved than ever knowing that he'd been keeping an eye on me.

I remained someone who took instructions or commitments literally, for most of my life; it seemed to be a way to please others, which I generally felt was a good thing to do. However, the downside is that I still find it too easy to feel let down when people don't fulfil their commitments to me, perhaps a trait of being a loyal person, but sometimes it can be a real burden to deal with.

My first friendships were with Mark and Kay, a boy and girl of similar age to myself, who lived close by. On the dirt track, located to the back of her garden, Kay and I sat facing each other, cross-legged with a carefully selected range of different size pebbles laid out before us. The idea was to see how big a stone I could ease into her nostril without it falling out. Needless to say, I eventually found one that fitted to perfection, after a bit of coaxing, resulting in Kay having to be taken to hospital to get it extracted. We remained friends, but it was around this time that I was encouraged to play with boys rather than girls.

Another pastime was when Mark and I would regularly rattle the front garden gate of a neighbour's house to tease their Boxer dog, which would then sprint from the rear garden to try to get to us. The bounding hunk of muscle would approach at great speed, before being confronted by the secure wooden gate and fencing, allowing us time to taunt the dog further, before casually walking off home. However, one particular time the owner had obviously had enough of our after-school visits, when he left the gate ajar. Suddenly and without warning the ferocious beast was bounding straight for us, at the time when we noticed the gate to be unlocked. The adrenalin rush was immense as we began our sprint to a special hideaway which was located on a nearby street, just below the crescent that we were making our escape from. Previously, the hideaway was always used as a sort of sanctuary, consisting of a dug-out hollow, two feet below pavement level in the centre of a substantial privet hedge.

Leaping in to the security of the den, I turned around to be confronted with the boxer's grumpy face, staring straight at me. His salivating, gnashing mouth was just inches away from my face when he decided to lunge, taking a firm bite of my left arm as he did so. Fortunately, my anorak saved me from any permanent damage, but the shock of the confrontation made me freeze with fear. As the dog ran off, I began to come to terms with the consequences of my actions, a realisation that I'd escaped serious injury. I knew after this experience that I would never bother 'Cuddles' again. How ironic that when I'm asked what my favourite dog is I always say a Boxer, making me wonder if there's some deep-seated guilt inside of me, wanting to make up for the misery that I put that poor animal through.

Once, I found a stray hedgehog wandering on the road; its slow, aimless actions implied that it was injured. I was saddened to see the creature in such distress, yet at the same time excited, as it was the first time that I'd ever seen such an animal. The spikes on its body felt as prickly as sewing needles, making it impossible to pick up, particularly when it rolled up into a ball to protect itself. My solution was to collect some long grass to wrap around its body, allowing me to gather the creature into my cupped hands.

I kept my new pet in a rusty tin bath, previously thrown out into the back garden, and I felt highly encouraged to know that I'd saved the life of this beautiful animal. I sometimes felt under pressure to release my pet, when Mum and Dad told me that it might have ticks or fleas, but my instincts told me that I should continue to look after it. Visits to see the hedgehog were regular over the next few days, when I would leave supplies of grass with a dish of fresh milk for it to feed on. However, one day it wasn't there, and I naively concluded that it had climbed up the smooth tin walls of the bath to make its escape to live a life of luxury somewhere in the overgrowth.

Many years later I discovered that hedgehogs weren't vegetarian by choice, that the grass I left for it to feed on would have done very little to aid its recovery, and I came to the conclusion that my parents had released it. I looked inquisitively at my parents, questioning them but without ever getting a clear answer about my concern, but the incident had conveniently become a fading memory to them.

Passing time with friends always seemed to involve new challenges, incidents, and pushing boundaries. Even as a six-year-old it was accepted that I could play outside unsupervised, so long as I didn't stray into the quarry. On hot sunny days most of the boys in the neighbourhood ventured out from the security of their homes on to the streets to play, as it was considered to be a safe place. Very few cars were ever seen on the estate and the rag-and-bone man would always give you plenty of warning that he was in the vicinity, shouting loudly, 'any old iron,' as he approached on his horse and cart. We were always happy to recycle metal or any other items of consequence, as our reward was to select a balloon from a multi-coloured pack, something we rarely saw otherwise.

It was on such a day that a group of us had gathered outside on the pavement, when peer pressure was placed on several of us younger boys to relocate to a side of the quarry edge. We spotted a gang of lads playing on the basin floor of the site, then without warning or hesitation, some of our group began to throw stones at the sitting targets a couple of hundred yards below us. As a gesture of loyalty, I half-heartedly threw a stone, setting off running before it had barely left my hand, fear gripping me as I did so. As far as I was concerned, I was now sprinting for my life, leaving the rest of the group trailing behind me.

I approached a well-trodden pathway that led to our escape route, through Mark's back garden, a track that we often used when coming home from school. However, this time I was panic-stricken as I sprinted frantically towards the boundary embankment. In my haste I tripped, then fell head first, hitting my head on the corner of a brick that was protruding out of the ground, with the impact stunning me. As I regained composure, blood began to trickle down from a gash to my forehead, allowing a friend to catch up with me and offer me support as I shuffled home, tearful and mumbling. It wasn't until I saw my parents that I began to sob uncontrollably, before being taken to hospital, where I had ten stitches to repair the wound.

As well as experiencing exciting, sometimes dangerous times, the quarry also served up some loving memories. For several days, on the way home from school, I picked bunches of beautiful pink, rose bay willow herb (fireweeds) which made my mother's lovely face beam. I never did quite understand when, some time later, she gently told me that she'd got enough flowers for now and didn't want any more for a while. It seemed that my daily selection of weeds was getting larger by the day, making it impractical to have them on show any longer.

Playing out one day, I was lured to investigate several large, concrete drainpipes that had been tipped on the quarry floor, measuring around four-feet in diameter. "Get in Glyn and we'll make a den," said one of the boys as they began to block off each end of the eight-foot-long pipe. As the second wooden board was put in place, darkness enveloped me and the anxiety became overwhelming, now realising that I'd been trapped, inside the cylinder. The older boys laughed more and more as a response to my screaming and kicking to be let out, and some moments later, with energy reserves now totally expended, I managed to escape. I can think of no explanation, other than the boys must have taken pity on me, when they eventually began easing the supports that were holding the timber sheets in place, before running off. My relief was palpable as the daytime sunlight eventually broke through into the grim tomb.

Some forty-seven years later, when I was fifty-two years old and living in Kettering, I found myself being assessed for a neck injury and an appointment was made to visit a portable MRI unit that was sited at the nearby private hospital. After handing over my details to the nurse, I was asked to lay down on my back, before being manoeuvred into the machine head first. The top of the x-ray unit was only a few inches away from my face, a snug fit to say the least, and as the hatch was shut closed, my anxiety levels rose. Such was the tension that counting down the seconds for the ten-minute ordeal seemed the easiest way to get through the scan, and then having to repeat the action after being told that I'd moved during the process! Although I didn't think about my entrapment in the drain, subconsciously, it may have triggered the anxiety that I felt from that time, making me almost cancel the procedure.

In due course and in preparation to start a new term at Bole Hill Junior School, our family moved home to the district of Walkley, into a Victorian end-of-terrace property that operated as the local corner shop. The small business was carried on by my parents for a while, offering basic convenience products such as vegetables, cheese and a small selection of branded, packaged goods. Our primary living accommodation was the back-reception room, with a poorly equipped, galley-type kitchen adjacent to it, measuring no more than nine feet long by four feet wide. Moving into a privately owned property was a big step forward for my parents as we were now expected to fully support ourselves, having always relied on government-built council houses up to this time. We didn't have a bathroom or internal toilet facilities at our new home, so in reality the purchase was a step backwards, as far as comfort was concerned. My weekly bath took place in a metal tub which was placed on the kitchen floor, before being topped up with hot water previously boiled to temperature on the primitive gas cooker.

Day-to-day washing was generally with a cotton flannel dipped in cold or hot water depending on whether the kettle had been boiled earlier for a brew. It was a rushed and torturous ordeal during the winter months, and Mum would frequently carry out a hygiene inspection, checking behind my ears and under my arms for grime. Our toilet was in a block, some twenty-five yards away from the house, via a pathway that accessed the back doors to the adjoining row of terraced homes, with the small, elevated gardens retained by a substantial brick wall, overlooking the neighbour's driveway below us.

I created a new game that required me to lean over the top of the wall, from the highest point, then stretch over to see how far down I could reach with my right hand. I felt that the time had come to try and beat my previous record, but I overstretched! The inevitable happened and I found myself falling head first towards the ground from twelve feet, with no other choice but to brace myself for a heavy landing on to the pathway below. As I lay there motionless, unable to breathe, I suddenly let out a loud shriek as part of my recovery from a severe winding. Mrs Wilson, our neighbour from the house below, had been watching the saga unfold from her front lounge window and it was she who was the first on the scene. As I slowly recovered from my breathlessness, Mum appeared wanting to know what had "gone on!" In her broad Yorkshire accent, Mrs Wilson told her that "A thought he couldn't stretch much moor over wall, wee out hurting him-sen!" I hobbled off, only slightly worse for wear.

We regularly popped over the road to Nan and Grandad's on Sunday afternoons for our roast chicken meal, and as soon as I entered the house the smell of the food overwhelmed the senses. It wasn't long before Nan would offer me a cup of boiling hot gravy, made up from the giblets, some vegetables, with a slab of beef lard added to increase the quantity required for a pre-lunch tipple! The rest of the 'liquid gold' was used on the copious amounts of hot Yorkshire pudding, which was always served up by itself as a starter. Apparently, the tradition was that Yorkshire pudding would be served as both a hot starter and cold dessert, ensuring that stomachs were always full. The flat, doughy slab, with dark, crispy, raised edges would be cut into rectangular portions, and then served with jam or treacle. Fortunately, by the time I was old enough to understand what I was eating, times had moved on, with meat becoming more affordable, and smaller, individual puddings were being served primarily as a starter with gravy. My dad would sometimes have the Yorkshire pudding as a cold tea-time snack, but desserts were almost unheard of in our household, other than Sunday evenings when we might have canned fruit cocktail with Carnation cream.

During my time in the Royal Navy, three friends came home with me for a weekend trip, and after Sunday lunchtime drink with my dad, we arrived back to the house, where Mum had been preparing Sunday lunch. There seemed to be unlimited amounts of Yorkshire pudding being served up with lashings of gravy, and I couldn't believe what I was hearing, as one by one my friends gratefully accepted Mum's invitation for them to have seconds, then thirds of the starter. I was comfortably recognised as the 'hoover' out of the group, but even I'd declined seconds on this occasion, so big were the portions that were being served. As the saga unfolded, they all looked at me with a vacant expression before saying that they thought the Yorkshire puddings were the main course. My reputation as the 'hoover' was happily retained, as I gratefully demolished their leftover portions of chicken and veg after eating my own!

I suddenly became conscious about my personal appearance as I approached my teenage years. My hair was unusually straight, incredibly shiny with a double crown that would not allow my hair to be forced into any other style than where it naturally lay. Hair products, except for Brylcreem, were expensive, and basic barber shops were far more common than hair stylists, so my options were to like it or lump it. With the family's financial limitations, it was left up to Mum to cut my hair with what can only be described as an instrument of torture, comprising a long-handled, double-sided razor which was usually blunt, obvious by the brown rust showing on the edges of the blades. This weapon would be dipped in water then it would tear through my hair, causing me to jolt with the pain from the scalping that I was receiving! Occasionally, my high-pitch squeals were met with attempts to calm me by Mum asking me to stop moving or she might ruin my hairstyle, a comment that raised a knowing smile from both of us!

From the age of ten I began to realise how physically powerful I'd become, coinciding with being bullied or antagonised for no apparent reason other than boys were beginning to push limits, but I soon discovered that fear made me impervious to pain. It was a rarity to be taken shopping for new clothes, as most, if not all of the family's clothing came from Mum's regular trips to local church jumble sales. After one such trip she convinced me that I looked smart in a blue, chunky, knitted jumper that had rainbow-coloured speckles interweaved through it, finished off with three large buttons to one side of the neck line! I reluctantly wore the garment to school the following day, genuinely embarrassed at how I looked, with my face glowing pink! Nick and Phil, who were in my class, began taunting me incessantly, telling me that the jumper looked like a girl's blouse! The fact that I knew it was gave me very little reason to dispute their taunts and it wasn't long before they began to make the most of my shy vulnerability. These two boys were stylish, had the coolest hairstyles and always had lots of girls scribbling their names on the school desks, an early form of graffiti that was testament to how adored you were by the opposite sex. Throughout the lunch break they persisted in goading me, until they eventually pushed me too far. Nick was recognised as the hardest lad in the junior school; he was a tall, handsome boy but always very grumpy and this aggressive trait created an aura of toughness, that no-one dare challenge for as long as I knew him. Phil was Nick's sidekick whose bark was always worse than his bite, but he always seemed quick to spot any weakness in people! As the bullying intensified, so my adrenalin levels increased, to such an extent that my overtly aggressive reaction caught them by surprise and I put Nick on the floor with just one punch. He seemed content to stay there holding his face, whilst Phil looked like a scared rabbit as he ran off, with a cowardly, sheepish look on his face, telling me that I was now 'in the s**t!' I was left shaking and crying as the adrenalin continued to build, only subsiding when the dinner ladies became involved, eventually coming to the conclusion that I'd been picked on. I was challenged again by these two boys some months later, but I stood my ground, causing them huge embarrassment and I was never intimidated by them again.

Our family moved house again, bringing us to Fern Road, where a stretch of woodland broke up the landscape between our home and a small dam in the bottom of Rivelin Valley. What a playground this was for an eleven-year-old boy, but like anything in life, if you don't respect something it can come back to bite you! The densely planted spinney was made up of mature deciduous trees – mostly oak – which became a temptation to climb, and when ascending I had a tendency to keep both eyes on the sky above, without much concern for how high I'd ventured! However, when it came to descending from the trees, my nerve seemed to desert me when I looked down, resulting in some hair-raising experiences. The first time this happened, I was shuffling along a branch in the prone position to loop a rope around it, which, if successful would have enabled my friends and I to make our own swing. I was guided to the point where I needed to be, then looked down before freezing with fear, but as my grip slackened, I overbalanced, before falling to the floor in an undignified manner, the impact cushioned by the prickly stalks of the blackberry bushes below.

Some months later I found myself halfway up the mother of all oaks when a passing youth began to verbally abuse me from below, whilst his girlfriend stood there smiling, particularly when he began throwing stones in my direction. I gripped the tree with all my might as several more missiles whizzed past my head, some bouncing off the branches around me and I was so relieved when he decided to move on, after losing interest in using me as a target. My frustration and anger in not being able to get some sort of revenge, resulted in a precarious descent as tears glazed over my eyes, and it was to be the last time that I ventured up a tree of any size.

I wish I'd stopped climbing trees a few years earlier, as it would have prevented me from severely injuring myself on an insignificant elder tree! The event started off well enough, when a group of us had congregated on some wasteland to the rear of a friend's house, before going into a derelict shed to light a fire for a laugh! I didn't want to be implicated in the wrongdoing and I was immediately drawn to a tree, but little did I know that the branches were very weak and mostly brittle. Within seconds, I'd fallen from no more than four feet, the broken branch that I'd been standing on piercing my left-hand side like a dagger, as I slumped to the floor. There was no blood from the wound and I lay on my back peacefully, with no pain but in a daze, until help came. Once home I remember pleading for a drink of water, but two police officers, who'd arrived before the ambulance, advised Mum not to give me any for the time being!

The ordeal left me requiring twenty-five stitches to close a circular gap that was sliced into the skin just above my waist line. Memories of my friend's father rushing me home whilst I lay in the back of his car stand out, as well as a blue-light ambulance ride, together with a police escort to the children's hospital. My mum was frantic with worry, concerned about the outcome of the injury and any lasting ill effects, but fortunately the branch had missed piercing any of my vital organs. After spending the next four weeks in hospital, I was eventually allowed home with no long-term problems, the trauma becoming a fading memory as the weeks passed by.

Another evening, a bunch of us went to Hillsborough Boxing Club to see what it was all about, but we quickly discovered that there was only boxing on offer (what did we expect). I was asked if I'd like to spar but I politely declined the request, infuriating one of the regulars at the club. The brazen heavyweight had already taken a dislike to me, telling me on several occasions that I should box him, before then trying to intimidate me, but I was in no mood to get my nose punched. Feeling threatened and becoming more nervous the longer we stayed around, it was a welcome relief to get out of the building to go home, but the boxer decided to follow us, yelling foul language and calling me a coward, at the same time as my friends taunted me to take him on. Nan's words of wisdom (or madness), about never backing down from a fight crept into my mind, convincing me that I couldn't walk away from the situation and I turned off the main road down a side street, which was partially lit from a street lamp. It was only a matter of seconds before he'd fronted up ready to fight, then began stepping forward towards me, and just like Nick some months earlier in the school playground, I floored the bully with one powerful punch to the face. He accepted defeat without any hesitation, but seemed totally shocked by what had happened to him as he eventually got up from his backside. I didn't hang around and rushed home after sensing my emotions getting the better of me and not wanting my friends to see me upset.

Some weeks later I was due to start at Myers Grove Comprehensive School, a place where almost two thousand children were being taught. It was probably these two well-documented fights that prevented further bullying throughout my time at senior school, as the boys that I fought were both in my year group, with the recognition of being the toughest lads from their respective schools.

I have never felt inclined to verbally exaggerate my mental or physical toughness, realising that there is always someone bigger or stronger around any corner. However, it strikes me that some people need to be stood up to, and bullies will often prove to be cowards when they're confronted, but it takes a brave, courageous soul to do so. I would now choose to step away from an aggressive situation or defuse confrontation with thoughtful words, if the need ever arose, but I've learnt that controlled aggression can prove very productive when participating in sporting events. To walk away from confrontation should be promoted as a sign of strong character, rather than a weakness, but all too often foolish pride blinds us into thinking that cynical aggression is the only solution to a problem. I thank God that I have learnt to enjoy and have a better understanding of humility, an emotion that shows up stubborn pride for the menace it can be.

In 2013-14, as a voluntary street pastor, my skills to defuse situations with words, humility and showing understanding were tested from time to time. On one particular occasion, two brothers and their partners had been leaving a pub, when it was alleged that a door man had groped the backside of the smaller brother's fiancé. Four of us were standing close by the entrance to the pub when a commotion started and we began to engage with the disgruntled boyfriend, but this served to fuel his bravado even more. It became as amusing as it was serious when his girlfriend told us how he got so jealous over nothing when he'd had a drink. She explained that he had a need to show her how much he loved her by getting stroppy with other men, but relied on his much tougher brother to sort things out if it got out of hand! I asked his girlfriend if she minded if I tried a particular ploy to calm him down and she agreed, but with some reservation. I talked to the man, asking what he was going to do to the bouncer, as I carefully unwrapped one of the sweet lollipops that I carried around in my pockets. Placing the lollipop in his mouth, he instantly took hold and began licking it at the same time as his temper subsided, his cursing and swearing ceased, and a smile appeared on his face. His response was "Well, this doesn't look f***g hard licking this, how can I fight with this in my gob!". We all burst out laughing and the incident was diffused, ending with the four of them getting a taxi home.

During my early senior school years, I was a happy boy, developing new friendships and adapting well to the expectations required of me being in one of the top classes. However, as we settled in to our new home in Fern Road, there was a period that I heard my parents regularly complaining between themselves about a smell in the lounge! For some inexplicable reason, I convinced myself that I was the cause of their concern and that it was me that was creating the odour. This ridiculous assumption led me to fits of crying whilst out of sight, at the same time holding a cutlery knife to my stomach, daring myself to press harder and harder as some sort of penance for what I was putting them through. How or why these emotions came and went, I'm unsure, but the sad memory remains and nothing remotely similar has ever happened to me since. I've had cause to re-evaluate this incident most recently, from a Christian perspective, and my conclusion is that the smell coincided with a time when my friends and I innocently played Ouija in the house, a game where spirits are called to direct an empty glass across a board which would spell out answers to your questions! Alison and I have been leaders of our church's prayer ministry team since 2008, and I now have total confidence and experience of overcoming any ungodly activity by praying in Jesus' name. But, at the time, and without a Christian faith, perhaps my friends and I had actively encouraged inappropriate, supernatural activity within my parents' home, something the Bible wholeheartedly discourages.

There was a small reservoir at the bottom of the woods near where we lived, which had a shingle-covered area to one side that was ideal for cars to park up or boys to test out their various cycling skills. I didn't have a pedal cycle at the time, but l was fascinated to see how everyone was skidding sideways like the speedway stars on TV. I asked a boy if he'd show me how to do the same, keen to learn in case I ever managed to convince my parents to buy me my own set of wheels at some time. The boy seemed excited by the attention I'd afforded him, quick to pass his 'cow horn handle bar' bike over to me in readiness to have a go! This sort of model tended to be made up from parts of several other discarded bikes, with wide-angled handlebars protruding from the main stem, ideal for off-road activities or heavy-duty play. He explained that I needed to pedal as hard as I could to reach my optimum speed before slamming on the back brake, and after receiving further instructions, I set off powerfully in front of a small audience. As I reached top speed, I instinctively began turning the front wheel, whilst simultaneously slipping my left foot in to the gravel and squeezing the right-hand brake lever; but this proved to be a serious mistake, as it engaged the brake pads to the front-wheel rim rather than the back wheel! The boy had set me up for a painful fall! I'd never taken much interest in ballet, but I learnt that there was more than one version of the 'nutcracker suite'. As the cycle stopped dead, my feet shot forward off the pedals, at the same time as my rear end left the saddle, and with great pace my private parts slammed into the upright support stem of the handle bars as I threw my hands up in the air. I ran along with the bike for a split second before crumpling head first into the sharp shingle, the bike catapulting over me as I lay spreadeagled in the prone position! Only my pride was seriously hurt, but I still managed to retain a smile as my friends creased up with laughter at what they'd just witnessed.

Three years later, aged fourteen, I was able to afford a second-hand pushbike costing £3. The lump of metal looked the part, having cow bar handles, or 'ape hangers' as we called them, with only one gear, accompanied by the additional feature of inoperable, worn down brakes. During this period, Mum worked overtime at the local jumble sales to keep finding me shoes as the soles were being worn through with great haste, due to them becoming my main tools for braking. It was with this same bike that Steve and I ventured out to Bradfield on one of our longer cycle rides, and reaching the outskirts of the village, we began our descent down a steep hill. It had been raining for some time, the roads becoming slippery from the heavy, ongoing downpour, when Steve encouraged me to go for it, pressing the point that I had a good pair of shoes on my feet! Easy for Steve to say when he had a cycle that had three gears, with all the mod cons and an operational braking system! I set off with some trepidation, marginally behind my friend, overtaking him as soon as he applied his brakes at the first corner, my confidence growing as I began freewheeling at top speed with my legs outstretched either side of the bike, acting like stabilizers. It was a great feeling to be in full flow, unconcerned about danger, even though I found myself sometimes straying on the wrong side of the country road and as I exited a bend, the brake lights of a Mini lit up in front of me. It was an exhilarating moment speeding past the car, gasping nervously as I first held my breath in anticipation of a collision, but eventually coming to a natural halt at the bottom of the village. I decided that trying to master my skidding techniques, in the relative safety of the car park of the local dam, was a far safer option from then onwards!

I discovered just how deep the dam was when my friend, Robert, persisted in poking a wasp's nest with a stick, located a few yards away from the water's edge. We'd already discussed the various options open to us if the wasps decided to attack, but none of them seemed that great to me, plus I'd not taken any interest in disturbing the creatures, thinking that it was both unnecessary and cruel. I therefore paid him lip service, before moving some distance away from the danger area as he continued antagonising them. The moment arrived when the wasps decided they'd had enough and began swarming towards us at great speed, a footpath being our only means of escape. With a stealth bomber's precision, the swarm seemed to know who to attack and locked on to its target, and without hesitation Robert plunged in to the freezing cold water, screaming as he did so. He bobbed up and down in the water to take breath before the creatures eventually retreated, allowing him to crawl out of the water to show us several sting marks as his badge of honour.

During that same summer holiday period, again led by Robert, we toiled for hours to bring a disused bathtub upstream from Loxley Valley, back to the local dam. We convinced ourselves that this vessel would definitely float, with all four of us in it! Our exhaustion became a fading memory when we entered the last stretch of the river, nearest our proposed destination. A small artificial ledge had been formed around the perimeter of the dam, just below the water line; this allowed us to balance one end of the bath into the water's edge, without being fully immersed. However, as soon as the tub's elevation moved forward, the waste drainage hole allowed water to flow in, overbalancing then submerging the fibreglass cast. "Quick, jump in!" was the command, which saw Colin and I leap in to the unstable bath, only to speed up the inevitable sinking of the vessel. We both swam out of the water giggling, much to Robert's annoyance, as he demanded that we go back in to recover the boat! The weight of the water-filled bath was too much for any of us to successfully recover, leaving our leader rather disgruntled!

Colin was Robert's younger brother, who seemed to respond to Robert's demands, even when the requests seemed mischievous. However, I would make an excuse to get away from them when I felt it necessary. One bright and sunny evening we were heading back home, after having good fun playing in the Donkey Woods, when it was suggested that we all went scrumping for apples in someone's garden just around the corner from where we lived. Instead, I opted to climb a tree located on wasteland just across from my home, which seemed to aggravate Robert intensely, prompting him to begin swearing, and threatening to drag me off the branch that I was sitting on. I still refused to budge even though he continued to antagonise me, his rage eventually getting the better of him, as he began moving closer. I realised what his plans were so I stood up on the large branch ready for his next move, and as his chest became level with my feet, he pulled his arm back in an attempt to strike me. I began to kick out, forcing him to stumble to the ground as the ferocity of the attack caught him out. He ran off to catch up with the others but not before threatening that he'd get me back another day. I jumped down from the tree, sprinted home, and then began crying uncontrollably in front of my parents. My Dad's response was predictably unsympathetic as he began laughing awkwardly, explaining that it should have been Robert that was crying, not me.

For several days I lived in fear of his threat of retribution, before Colin divulged that his Dad had told his brother that if he touched me, then his Dad would punish Robert. When the need arose, they both still received punishment by being smacked across their backside, with their father's leather belt. Needless to say, Robert never intimidated me again and it was their Dad who three years later and only one week before I was due to join the Royal Navy said, in his strong Yorkshire accent "Tha'll never last, in't Navy."

Our first family holiday with Nan and Grandad Hill was to a holiday camp called Scalby Mills, located on a cliff top overlooking Scarborough Bay. My grandad, Ernest, was the only driver in the family up to that time, so with great excitement we hired a car for the trip away. We were all immensely proud of him as he'd been awarded several medals for safe driving during his career. Mum often reminded us about Grandad's driving achievements, reiterating the point as we set off on our journey towards the east coast. It was the first time that I'd been in a car and it was jam-packed with clothing, four adults and two children, all wedged tightly together as we trundled along the country lanes. We began to near our destination when we found ourselves having to slow to a crawl, due in part to the number of tractors or caravans that we encountered. To be in a traffic jam, on a scorching hot day, gasping for air, was not my idea of fun, when all of a sudden, our car bumped the back of another vehicle, which had come to an abrupt halt in front of us. Fortunately, there was no damage to either car, only to Grandad's pride. Mum, struggling to hold back from bursting out laughing herself, still found the composure to gently tell me off for my outbreaks of laughter, in support of her now blushing father and as a way to alleviate any further embarrassment for him.

Whether it was on merit of good behaviour or a lucky dip I'm unsure, but I was once selected to play a musical instrument. But it may have seemed like a punishment for Paul, the smallest lad in class who finished up with a large baritone, whilst one of the tallest boys, myself, was chosen to play a small cornet! We eventually arranged to swap instruments and sometimes practised together, as he lived nearby. Unfortunately, playing rugby, having a giggle and sticky valves always seemed to get in the way of practising for any length of time but they persevered with me. The music department held an annual concert in the main hall of the school, and the orchestra was encouraged to invite their parents along. Mum was so proud of me, obvious by her beaming smile from within the crowd of onlookers, then free-flowing tears as we played her favourite hymn, 'Abide With Me'. Every time thereafter, when she spoke about how well we'd played, she would puff up with pride and have a tear in her eye. It was a couple of years later, having constantly performed poorly in music lessons when I built up the courage to ask my teacher if I could quit playing the instrument. I was given a lecture about letting people down etc., but my instructor eventually agreed, once he knew I had the backing of my parents after producing a letter from them. It was also time to come clean with Mum, explaining that I'd been so nervous at concerts that I just puffed out my cheeks in time with the music, pretending that I was actually playing the notes! She burst out laughing at the thought that she'd been duped, whilst forever remaining a 'proud mother', still telling friends about my musical achievements for many years afterwards.

Up to the age of twelve I'd not really been devoted to any particular musical genre. Instead, playing sport, messing about with my friends, and eating were my passions! I was eventually introduced to vinyl records when I was given an LP for Christmas called 'Top of the Pops' and was further enthralled to receive a portable record player – a real treat, second-hand or not! The 'Top of the Pops' albums were produced annually, as very basic cover versions of that particular year's greatest hits, and from memory the pretty women that adorned the front covers of the albums had far more appeal than the music ever did.

That same year, further record albums were given to me, the contributory factor being that it always followed a visit from Mum's usual midweek outing to a jumble sale. If I'd have managed to hold on to my purchases, the vinyl would be a collector's dream now, as many were original copies of early releases from the likes of the Beatles and Rolling Stones. At the time they were often mishandled, but listened to repeatedly, creating a new interest for me. I eventually developed a taste for 'Heavy Rock,' purchasing my first brand-new album many months later by Alice Cooper, called 'Billion Dollar Babies'. I went on to build up a steady record collection, broadening my range of sounds from T Rex to Deep Purple, Wings to Black Sabbath, with lots of other artists in between. I sold all my records to lads in the Navy, some years later, after discovering Motown and Soul.

One weekend, when I was twelve, I bumped in to a classmate called Phil, who was an interesting character but a little bit wild for my liking, and he asked me round to his house. As we walked down his side driveway, I observed some of his dad's engineering tools and mechanical equipment through the open door of the garage. The lawn was unkempt and over ten times the size of what I was used to, but I'd entered a new world and my mind began to wander. The elevated patio area, overlooking the green expanse, was now becoming my fort, World War Two bunker, or any number of other childlike fantasies that I was conjuring up in my mind, but what would I do if he asked me to repair his go-kart, which was in bits in the garage, or pass him tools that I hadn't even seen before? I was nervous, yet excited at the prospect!

It was therefore a shock when Phil mentioned that one of his chickens needed to be killed! Without hesitation, and encouraging me to do the same, he began chasing several free-range birds, which were now frantically scampering around the walled arena that was his garden. He was eventually successful in apprehending one of the lively creatures, the start of a nightmare scenario for me, as he began tugging at the chicken's head, warning me that it could come off in his hand if he pulled too hard. "You have a go, Glyn," he insisted, as I looked at him in horror, before dropping the bird the instant it was passed to me. The chicken was soon caught again, and this time there was no hesitation as Phil held the animal's body on the concrete drive, then began sawing off its head! I was instructed to place my foot on the bird, whilst he began to tidy up the mess, when my nerve let me down, my disgust at what I'd witnessed now tangible, as I immediately released my foot away from the decapitated body. Unbeknown to me, chickens tend to retain lots of energy after slaughter, a point proven when the headless body went berserk, flapping around at great speed before finishing up in the next-door neighbour's garden, which I took as my cue to make a quick exit!

Regrettably, within five years of this incident Phil had passed away, having been involved in a motorbike accident at the age of seventeen. For many years the front, half-glazed porch, which created a centrepiece to his parents' double-fronted house, was meticulously decorated with fresh flowers as a shrine to their beloved son. It was a timely reminder to my age group at the time, to live life to the full, but respect life for the beautiful gift that it is.

An old pal called Jonny invited me to attend Pathfinders youth club, a Christian organisation based in the district of Hillsborough. I was fourteen years old and the prospects of playing five-a-side football in the community centre each Friday evening, was enough to overcome my concerns about having to attend church once a month to retain my affiliation. A further attraction was that Debbie, a girl that I'd taken a fancy to at school, also attended the club, but which unfortunately turned out to be another misguided dream. The rules regarding church attendance weren't vigorously upheld, but it was definitely a time when my views of Christianity started to be challenged. I attended a couple of summer camps with the group, based on a site at Criccieth in Wales, and the two expeditions to the top of Mount Snowdon stand out as milestones, at the same time allowing me to discover that I had a stubborn side to my personality. I hated walking and the prospect of having to trek to the top of a mountain filled me with dread, so much so that on both occasions, when we reached the mountain-top cafe, I refused to venture to the summit, a short distance higher. It was to be another thirty years before my frustration resurfaced about not quite completing the trek to the very top of Snowdon, something I completed with my son, Rory, when he was only eight years of age. This time the trek was a thrilling adventure that we both thoroughly enjoyed, and which, to complete the final part to the summit, required us to crawl on our hands and knees over scree that was covered in ice and snow, whilst fog and gale force winds enveloped us. It will be a memory that I will always cherish, even if embarrassingly, Rory was in better shape than me by the end of it. I like to think that by successfully completing this feat, it became the main driving force behind our joint trek to Base Camp Everest in 2017.

One of our youth leaders at Pathfinders, called Martin, was a well-built, retired footballer, who was quite bold in letting us know that he was an ex-gang member. He seemed happy to tell us about how his exploits would frequently lead to 'gay bashing', which involved going to areas where gay men would gather, then mercilessly carrying out beatings to those suspected of being homosexuals. It was with this knowledge that I took on a small paid job to take his washing to the local laundrette in Hillsborough, each Friday evening prior to youth club starting. It was only a few days earlier that Jonny had packed in doing the reasonably paid task before asking if I wanted to take it on, something that I gratefully accepted. As I got to know Martin better, I had no reason to question his motives when he first asked me to dye my pale brown hair, black. Even though the request seemed extremely strange, my only thought was whether or not it would make me more attractive to the opposite sex, something that I quickly dismissed! Confidence in my image was only just beginning to develop in a positive sense and dying hair was considered to be a girl only thing, therefore totally unrealistic, a pure joke, in my mind.

Several weeks passed, when one Friday evening as I returned back with the dry clothing to his studio annexe, which was tagged on to the rear of the vicarage, we had a few minutes to spare before the youth centre needed opening up. It was this evening that he did something that led me to question his motives for many years afterwards. For no apparent reason he decided to pin me down on his double bed. I found myself being pushed on to my back, whilst he forced my legs either side of my head, a bit like the first sequence in carrying out a backward roll, before holding me down by lying on top of me, his vast weight pinning me into the covered mattress. I began to panic, unable to breathe properly, before he eased off, making light of his actions whilst verbally telling me about how easily he'd overpowered me, but still lying on top of me as he continued in conversation. I'd been frightened enough by this experience, so much so that I stopped washing his laundry thereafter, ever wary of him after this event and never telling anyone what happened, until very recently. It's no wonder we grow up with prejudice when actions like this happen to us, but I never stopped trusting people, sometimes to my detriment.

Alan, a friend from senior school and an ardent Emerson Lake and Palmer fan, was keen to become a rock drummer legend by the time he was sixteen. A year earlier, he asked me if I fancied going to see a concert at Sheffield City Hall, but with a twist! The twist was that we didn't have to pay! It turned out that Alan was part of a dedicated crowd of 'gate-crashers,' explaining that he got in to most concerts that he attended free of charge, with little effort or consequences for carrying out the unlawful act! It was only a matter of days before I donned my best gear, all of which came from jumble sales, and headed down town to meet up with him. The outfit consisted of a bright yellow corduroy Wrangler jacket, a plain T-shirt with baggy cords cut down to just above the ankle, with a sturdy pair of brown 'Doc Marten' boots. My first visit to the City Hall was to see Showaddywaddy, a band that attracted a full house of two-thousand people. The grand timber doors that served as fire exits around the old Victorian building were our first obstacles to gaining free entry, but a seasoned gatecrasher always seemed to appear at the right time, someone able to easily flip the security bar that locked the interlocking doors. The bravest boys led the way up the stairs, but it wasn't until the first lad got to the corridor that we knew whether security was on to us or not! It quickly became evident whether or not the effort had been worthwhile, resulting in a swift retreat or a dash into the arena and if it was the latter option, a great stampede would ensue, where it was then expected that every man would take care of himself.

It was my first concert and I'd successfully entered the auditorium, having managed to secure a seat in the top tier balcony and believing that I wouldn't be disturbed for the rest of the evening, as I settled down to enjoy the live performance. Without warning, two doormen appeared either side of the row of seats, then began running towards us, creating an explosion of bodies, all eager to disperse through the small exit doors that had been vacated by the bouncers. I got out of the building quicker than I'd got in, but I was left invigorated by the rush it had given me, making it an easy decision to meet regularly with Alan thereafter. Over the coming weeks I saw many live performances, my favourites being Lynyrd Skynyrd, Be Bop Deluxe and Ginger Baker, a world-renowned drummer as part of the Baker Gurvitz Army, but previously with Cream, but things came to a head when I tried getting in to see Black Sabbath. There was an unusual amount of people trying to crash the concert, most of them unknown to me, but they were far more aggressive than normal, challenging door staff and up for a fight if they were obstructed. Security was high, with police cars patrolling regularly after some violent incidents had been reported, when suddenly I found myself being chased by a police patrol car, which sent me into overdrive. I sprinted as fast as possible, then turned up a side street, flinging myself over a small dwarf wall which formed the frontage to a commercial property, where I was able to hide until I thought it safe to resurface. The reality was that the car was probably trying to disperse several of us from an area, but in my mind, he'd got his eye on me, which was enough to keep me away from the arena for a few weeks. It was getting more difficult to access the hall for big bands, and Marc Bolan's T Rex was another that I gave up on within half an hour of arriving. I learnt, many years later, that it just so happened to be a concert that my future wife, Alison, made a special trip from Nottinghamshire to attend, but she had the good sense to pay for her ticket!

Alan convinced me to return to the concert hall to see an artist that he described as being a rocker, his name, George Hamilton IV! We could have probably got free tickets for this event, if we'd have done our research on the artist properly! We eased into the hall through a favoured door that led to the top floor, before taking our seats in the empty balcony! It soon became evident that this was a concert for the more discerning, middle-age person, and most of the crowd was confined to the ground floor area, all sitting politely, whilst watching the veteran artist perform his greatest hit! George was singing away merrily when two doormen appeared by one of the exit doors, smirking at the five of us that had decided to attend the evening! We caved in after just a few seconds, as a way of saying that we'd 'cocked up,' and made our way to them as intense embarrassment got the better of us, before being marched to an office where we were questioned aggressively by the manager. I could feel my bottom lip start to quiver as I began to wonder what my parents would think of me, conscious that I could soon have a criminal record and that my world was beginning to turn upside down. The manager worked his way through us one by one, taking our names, addresses, the school we attended, plus a host of other questions that he demanded instant answers to. He abrasively pointed his finger directly at me, accusing me of being a regular at lots of concerts over the last few months and although my friend had already primed me to say that this was my first concert, if asked, the fumbled lie gave away how nervous I was. He grabbed my bright yellow corduroy wrangler jacket, along with my arm, before declaring that there must be lots of boys who own one of these! It certainly was a unique colour, blue denim Wrangler jackets being the purchase of choice at the time, if you could afford one. I never did hear any more about the incident, but it was a big enough shock to my system to stop me ever going back again, and thereafter I chose to pay to see artists like Ian Dury, Doctor Feelgood, Judas Priest and David Bowie.

It was supposed to be a special occasion when my parents allowed me to invite friends around for a small celebration on my sixteenth birthday. As the adults left for a night out, most of my pals had already arrived, but Mum's face was a picture when copious amounts of cheap alcohol appeared, then neatly stacked alongside the container of Watney's red bitter, previously purchased by Dad as a treat! With a naive confidence I was able to assure Mum and Dad that everything would be okay, but within two hours of their departure some older guys had arrived uninvited, one of which had previously told a girl that he was splitting up with her, whilst another was found testing out my bed, with his girlfriend alongside him. The noise levels were reaching a crescendo when unexpectedly the 'ditched girl' decided that it was a good idea to sit on our five-foot-high garden wall, with a clothes line wrapped around her neck. She was sobbing uncontrollably as several of us held on to her, gently coaxing the cable away from around her throat, before gaining control of the precarious situation. It was a relief to see her girlfriends come alongside and take her back home, as I abruptly brought the evening to a close. I must have asserted some sort of authority, as I managed to clear and tidy up the house before my parents returned shortly after 11pm, but it had been one of those occasions, that if status and finances had ever allowed it, the portrait oil painting of the master of the house would have been left sporting a felt tip moustache, or worse! I couldn't believe what I'd just witnessed, later promising my parents and myself that I would never hold such an event again.

Aged sixteen, a close friend called Stu, was already sporting bushy sideburns and shaving each morning before attending school. He comfortably looked eighteen and his physical development was way ahead of mine, and to put things into perspective I have never been able to grow facial hair of any substance to this day! A cinema called 'Studio 7' was notorious for hosting 'X-rated' movies, and it was mentioned by Stu that we should try and get in to see a film. My heart sank at the thought of watching a 'dirty movie' and I was already preparing my excuses to drop out. However, to my surprise, the film he wanted to watch was Enter the Dragon, a new release back then but now an iconic Kung Fu film featuring the legendary Bruce Lee. I convinced my parents that I wasn't doing anything too distasteful, even though it was classified for eighteen-year-olds and over, arguing that I would look old enough if I was allowed to wear my new jacket and trousers. The outfit had been made to measure and something that Dad had promised me for my sixteenth birthday, as my 'Coming of Age' present. Delighted to be given the green light, I entered Stu's house fully kitted out with shirt and tie to complement my new clothing, before politely been told that

I still looked really young! It was suggested that I should have grown some facial hair, ready for the trip out, but that was an impossibility. Approaching the cinema for the afternoon matinee screening, I became slightly nervous after being told to disguise my high-pitched voice with something a bit rougher, practicing what to say as the entrance doors got ever closer. To add further anxiety to the situation, Stu came up with a cunning plan and reaching into his jacket pocket, like magic, produced a tin of black polish! A fake moustache was added over my top lip, before entering the dimly lit reception area which helped to disguise the amateurish camouflage. It was left up to my friend to do all the talking at the kiosk, as I looked on over his shoulder, before taking our seats, then celebrating our triumphant admission to the empty auditorium.

My personality and principles made it difficult for me to be anything other than a well-behaved young teenager but as I sought new experiences, I resigned myself to the fact that this meant I would have to become a little naughtier. My rationale was that the so-called 'bad boys' always seemed to get away with their actions, and attracted the best-looking girls whilst having great fun in the process! However, I lived with a reverence for a God that I still didn't know or understand, but knew that my restlessness would have either led me to doing something rather stupid or dangerously extreme, so joining the Royal Navy proved an ideal compromise. It became a place that allowed me to discover new thrills and adventure within a relatively safe structure, and I looked forward to the challenge that it provided as I prepared to leave home in August 1976.

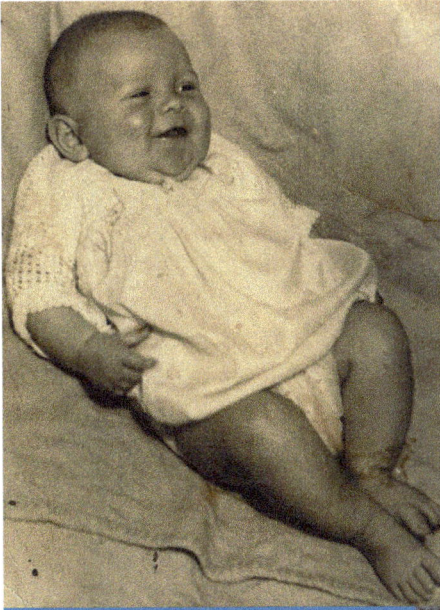

1960, Welcome to this world, Glyn!

Glyn and sister, Julie

(l. to r.) Dad, Auntie Mary, Mum, Nan and Grandad Wood

Glyn and Jonny, both 16; just before heading off to join the Royal Navy

(l. to r.) Nan Hill, Dad, Grandad Hill, Mum, Nan Wood & me. 1984

On holiday in Cornwall with my sister Julie and her husband Garry

Chapter Three

FAMILY BONDS

We moved to a house that also served as the corner shop on Bole Hill Road, Walkley, when I was six years old. The move brought us close to my dad's parents, and living just four doors away from Nan and Grandad Wood created a family bond that could only truly be appreciated and defined with hindsight. The closeness between us all taught me to take the rough with the smooth and, importantly, feel a strong sense of security having so many familiar adults around me. Nan was christened Harriet but was always known as Babs and worked part-time at the local bakers, and grandad, whose name was Bill, lived at home and was retired due to ill health. Mum ran the day-to-day management of the shop, whilst Dad would get up for work at 5.00am to catch the 5.45am bus to his workplace, as a store man at a steel distributor. His evening routine was to have his dinner as soon as he got home around 6.00pm, sleep for an hour, and watch television for the rest of the evening, before going to bed after eating a cooked supper, generally after 10.00pm.

Early memories of attending my Victorian junior school on Bole Hill Road, include being handed a small bottle of tepid milk that had been left outside in a crate. The rising sun often made the liquid congeal and further memories included; pretending to sing songs in assembly and having a slight crush on my teacher. There was a tiny strip of green field which was constantly 'out of bounds,' except for sports day and located above the top playground. However, I remember being assured that when we reached ten years old, we would be able to play football on the field, but it never happened and I felt very disappointed by the broken promise. At home I was encouraged to 'play out' at every opportunity, using my trendy black sneakers when playing footy on park land or spot-kicking a football against a wall with my mates, but white-washed plimsolls were later used for playing indoor sport at school. I was brought up on football, influenced by my father, who took me to a couple of Sheffield Wednesday games as a youngster, but excessive terrace hooliganism during the 1970s managed to turn him away from watching live games ever again, preferring instead to listen to match reports on the radio. I loved playing sport rather than watching it, but my main opportunity to play football until senior school, was either on the streets or at weekends when my friends and I would venture to the play park.

Another first was having toothache, not something you forget in a hurry once it takes hold. Oral hygiene wasn't a high priority in the 1960's, with limited use of fluoride being added in water supplies and none at all in toothpaste. However, it was probably the lure and temptation of free sweets, when we moved into the corner shop that set off my tooth decay. My first extraction was more akin to attending a butcher's shop rather than a dentist's practice, and the dental surgeon was eventually struck off for poor standards. The main anaesthetic for removing teeth was to inhale laughing gas through a mask, but he didn't give me enough, and failed to reapply the mask when I came around halfway through the extraction! I thought that I was having a nightmare at the time, where I was being held in a chair and a person was drilling through the back of my throat. The pain was excruciating and I'd been screaming frantically throughout, until someone came in the surgery, after my mum had complained to the receptionist. Fortunately, the tooth was already out as I slowly recovered from the effects of the gas and trauma.

My enthusiasm to play in a team was so great, that during my first week at comprehensive school I actively sought the sports noticeboard to find out what activities were available, where I spotted that the first training session of the week was for under-14s for the rugby team! I turned up with my whitewashed plimsolls, to be met by Mr Snell, a Physical Education teacher who keenly followed my rugby career through school, then long afterwards, before he passed away at a relatively young age. After being challenged about why I was at an under-14s session, I said that 'I was under 14.' His smile said it all as he made it clear to me that my age group was the under-12 team, which would be starting sporting activities the following week. I knew nothing about rugby but I was told to get a pair of boots, ready to train on the vast expanse of green pitches, which stretched far beyond the tarmac playground. I came home enthused by what I'd seen and heard, presenting Mum with a mission to find me a pair of football boots within the next few days! I knew no different, but a few days later my parents explained to me that the boots I was now holding in my hand, purchased from a jumble sale, would cover me for any field sport including rugby, football, hockey, cricket and athletics. The ankle-high boots had bright orange solid, toe-caps, that were potentially lethal weapons or at least a health and safety hazard, but no such safety regulations existed at the time! Not only were they lethal to anyone coming into contact with them, but I learnt very quickly that the panel pins, that held the solid studs in position to the outer sole, protruded through to the inner sole, constantly pricking the ball and heel of my delicate feet! I begged Mum to come up with a better pair of boots as a matter of urgency, only to receive a couple of cardboard cut-outs for the inner soles, as a first solution.

Dad always seemed content with his life, even though it sometimes meant him working overtime on Saturdays to top up his meagre wage, and it was during one of his Saturday morning shifts that he discovered that two foremen were thieving from their boss, having set up their own company not too far away from their employer's depot. I believe that my father's health suffered during this time through having to confront the situation as the main witness, an act that saved the company thousands of pounds, and his boss rewarded him with a meal for two at a restaurant of his choice! I later learnt that Dad had managed to spend £6 on his night out, treating Mum to their favourite dish of 'well done steak, chips and peas.' This was the same boss that some years later spent all of the staff's hard-earned pension money on propping up the company, leaving nothing for the employees when they reached retirement age. The saddest thing about this affair is that both my parents had to retire early, due to ill health, relying on government benefits with no comeback on Dad's wealthy boss.

The shop never really took off, but it did give my parents the impetus to better themselves and our next house move was to a pleasant, extended semi-detached property in Fern Road. We now had more living space than ever, with a landscaped wraparound garden to the side and rear of the property, but unfortunately, within a short period of time the mortgage payments had risen so high, that it made the property unaffordable. It was during this time my parents asked how I felt about moving to Australia, where job prospects seemed to be better. My parents' move abroad never came about and I doubt that they were ever serious, particularly as neither had previously ever wanted to travel much further than the east coast of England. However, a decision was made to downsize to a smaller, end-of-terraced house in Rivelin Street, where I lived until I left home in 1976, aged sixteen years and three months.

Being a well-behaved, considerate child came easily, having been taught to never answer back to anyone, to be seen and not heard, and to always respect my elders. But, as I reached my teenage years, I became shy and lacking in confidence, unwilling to engage in discussions for fear of an argument developing or that a fight may occur. I therefore allowed my frustrations to build up, eventually erupting in other ways, like regularly teasing my sister or reacting harshly when I reached boiling point, something that appeared totally out of character when it occurred.

Winding my sister up wasn't always a good idea as the consequences could be extreme! One such occasion occurred when I snatched a recorder off of her and began blowing into the mouthpiece, making a screeching noise rather than any musical contribution. I was sitting down at the time with the end of the instrument pointing upwards, when suddenly part of the recorder disappeared down my throat, together with a piece of a lower incisor tooth when Julie purposely smacked the end of the instrument with a book!

One of my regular duties was to escort her to the bus shelter at the top of the road and ensure that she got on the bus safely, as she was a lot younger than me. The bus would drop her off, a couple of miles away, close to where she took ballroom dancing classes. As we left the house one evening, I teased her so much that by the time we reached the shelter she was furious and swung at me with her laden bag. Fortunately, I ducked as the improvised weapon came towards my face, before connecting with a glass panel behind me which shattered into hundreds of tiny pieces. As I looked on in disbelief, her response was matter of fact and succinct, when she said "serves you right." The bus arrived in due course and, needless to say, I was able to hold this incident against her for several years afterwards!

Many more confrontations occurred after banging her 'Tiny Tears' doll on the floor, or dangling it upside down, making tears appear from a sump built into the toy's head. She saw this as an act of cruelty to her favourite possession but I would claim that I was just checking that the toy did as it said on the packet, spilling lots of tiny tears on demand! It was a welcome relief to learn that we had a love for each other rather than just tolerating each other, when a cessation of hostilities developed during my six weeks away from home whilst carrying out basic training in the Royal Navy. Many years on, I now feel that we have an even deeper relationship, due in part, to having lost all the older generations of family members that were linked to us. It is often during sad times when we are tested most, and I have found great comfort in discovering that, as well as having a lovely sister, I also have a close friend in Julie.

My only recollection of Grandad Wood spending time with me was before our move to Walkley, when he was a publican, at The Angel pub in Eckington. Grandad took me to the rear outbuilding to show me some beautiful bright yellow chicks that he'd recently purchased. The next time I saw the chicks was in the same building some months later, when they'd grown considerably and I watched his friend wring one of their necks. I didn't realise at the time, that the Sunday lunch I was eating some hours later, was the very chicken that I had just seen flapping and twitching, whilst being throttled up against the wall of the outhouse.

Grandad was a tall but physically fragile man, for as long as I knew him, with short grey hair and a harsh weathered face giving away his upbringing. He needed a walking stick to get around, was often found gasping for breath, bad-tempered and would begin to shout, swear and wave his walking stick when he became agitated. I took him in my stride because Nan would always stand up for me, challenging his attitude as he got more annoyed, something that seemed to be a regular occurrence. He never ventured very far from the house but could be seen taking in the fresh air regularly, sitting on a cushion on his front wall whilst chatting to his neighbour, Mr Cotton, another stern man. His favourite pastime was showing me some old coins that he kept in his pocket, the images so badly worn, that the faces were difficult to identify which era or date they represented. Grandad insisted that they were 'very old and worth a bit,' but we recently had a clear-out and sold the coins for £3.50 to a collector!

Nan and Grandad's Victorian two-up, two-down terraced house had a lounge that was grandly furnished compared to the kitchen-diner, but it was only ever used for special occasions, and one such event was when some of our relations were invited around each year for a meal just before Christmas. Nick was the same age as me but seemed far more educated, judging by his posh accent and having had a rural upbringing at a small village school called Todwick, on the outskirts of the city. Nick's father, Ken, had been unofficially adopted by Nan and Grandad as a child, remaining in a close relationship with them ever since and treated like a second son for most of his life. It was always the highlight of the evening when it came to selecting our drinks, and as the drinks' cabinet was opened it revealed an array of brightly coloured spirit bottles with mixers, cocktail umbrellas and plastic, multi-coloured sabre swords for piercing the glazed cherries, that must have been out of date! From a young age, Nan introduced me to a drink called a snowball, made from Warninks Advocaat, then heavily diluted with lemonade, and it became an annual treat thereafter.

During our last week of basic training in the Royal Navy, our class of twenty-four recruits was allowed out of barracks for a celebration. The destination was to be a nearby pub that had been previously vetted by the class leader, as a place that would allow under-age naval trainees on the premises. We were all dressed in full naval uniform and given a stern warning to be back on time and not to get drunk, so with haste we headed for the venue. On arrival, we were ushered towards a private area adjacent to the bar, before our orders were taken. As the pints of bitter and lager were being passed around, the place fell silent as a request for a Warninks Advocaat came through from the fresh-faced Yorky, sitting quietly in the corner. The language was blue; the laughter deafening as the three-inch-high, thimble-shaped, ladies' glass was handed over to me! The thick, yellow glutinous liquid created lots of attention and is still my favourite tipple today, an obvious Christmas present that still brings a smile to my face each time I receive a bottle.

After Nan had poured out the Christmas drinks, Nick and I would be left alone as the adults retired to the kitchen, allowing us to move an elaborate coffee table to one side of the room that created a miniature boxing ring, with nowhere to hide. The aged settee with its sturdy, plump cushions was a welcome sight, as whenever we got tired it was comforting to know that we had a soft base on which we could recuperate. Nan presented us both with a pair of aged boxing gloves, brought down from a wardrobe hideaway ready for their annual airing. The antiquated gloves appeared so large, having been made of a brown leather outer casing, then packed out with horsehair, or something similar, and although the leather appeared well worn, the construction of the glove was solid. The protruding thumb pieces looked enormous; nonetheless they embraced my thumbs like a vice and seemed heavy on my arms. We were both expected to have good fun battering each other and told 'not to get carried away', with an understanding that injury should be avoided at all costs! However, she would always discreetly remind me to give him 'a good poshing!' or beating, but the fighting generally stopped due to Nick getting exhausted after complaining of an asthma attack. I liked Nick, enjoyed my times with him but I was upset when one Christmas, Auntie June came into the lounge accusing me of being a bully, furious with me for hurting her son! I was beginning to get stronger, more powerful and on this occasion, I made Nick's nose bleed. Once again, my Nan stuck up for me, arguing that he was bigger than me, the assumption being that he should therefore be tougher than me!

Nan regularly reminded me that I should never take a step back if I ever got into an argument or fight, but then in the same breath that it was better to be a live coward, to fight another day, rather than to be a dead hero. Her advice was very contradictory but for many years, I only remembered to never step back in a fight and this advice, mistakenly, made me feel that when someone disagreed with what I did, said or thought, they wanted confrontation or an argument. I therefore had no concept of what a debate or discussion looked like, as school policy was similar to my family viewpoint about respecting your elders and never answering back! Like my father before me, I tried my best to avoid any decision-making, or be involved in any sort of dispute or deep discussion for fear of upsetting someone, and my shyness often got the better of me particularly when chatting to girls. Consequently, aged fifteen years old, it was a welcome relief to discover that drinking alcohol raised my confidence levels, enough to encourage conversation generally disguised as banter, rather than giving views that were too deep or wise!

It was in 1971 that I began attending Myers Grove Comprehensive School when, during a lesson, a teacher entered my classroom requesting that I go to Grandma's house immediately. I was offered no further explanation, other than my parents were waiting for me there. I rushed back, a little concerned, not knowing that Grandad had been ill for a few days. I was met by Mum and Dad and we moved upstairs to the main bedroom where Grandad lay, and the atmosphere seemed depressingly sombre. The family doctor listened to his chest through a stethoscope, whilst Nan pleaded with Bill to cough up the thick phlegm that could be heard rattling as he gasped for breath. Nan's anxiety was evident as she did her best to make her husband as comfortable as possible, but without much response from him, and as the doctor prepared to leave, he spoke to the adults. Nan was clearly upset with whatever he'd said and it was the last time that I recall seeing Grandad alive.

Grandad smoked up to 20 Woodbine cigarettes a day, from a very young age, having been a market trader for many years, before becoming a publican some time later. As a market trader he would be finished work by 10.30am, so would then drink himself into oblivion at a nearby pub. His mates would carry him into the back of his cart, before slapping the rear end of the horse to force it to trot off. The horse managed to get him home each day, which was several miles away, where Nan would put him to bed, sometimes soaking wet and after giving him a 'good rollicking'. Later on, as joint-tenants of The Angel pub, Nan regularly implied that Bill had drunk all of the profits that they'd ever made. She claimed that he spent every evening playing darts or singing around the piano with his friends, whilst she was left to do all the donkey work like cleaning and washing up. One evening, she was left to count up the takings for the night when the till jammed, making it impossible for her to close it securely. Attempting to tease the tray from the main body of the till, she found that a substantial quantity of ten-shilling, £1 and £5 notes were wedged to the rear of the tray and blocking up the sliding mechanism. She became elated, her face beaming every time she told me this story, so pleased as she explained that she'd kept all of the unaudited money to herself, without Grandad ever finding out. Her excuse for doing such a thing was that at times she was given so little cash to purchase essentials that she struggled to make ends meet, making the extra cash a real blessing to obtain additional food and treat herself.

Nan joked, that one evening she'd got into a serious fight with

Grandad after he returned home drunk and argumentative, resulting in her smashing a ceramic plant pot over his head! She stressed that he deserved what he got, going on to explain how the mixture of flowers, soil and blood that trickled down his face, had brought a sudden realisation that she'd overstepped the mark. As the fear embraced her she fled upstairs, locking herself in the bedroom until he'd calmed down. Fortunately, there were no further repercussions, perhaps a realisation for Bill, that he'd finally met his match. I didn't ever doubt that Nan had hurt Grandad in this way, as when she watched the wrestling on ITV's World of Sport on Saturday afternoons, she became a raging bull, shouting and gesturing wildly at the black and white television screen. Her minute stature, a little over five feet tall, hid a will and determination that made her a force to be reckoned with. She particularly disliked the antics of Mick McManus and Big Daddy, but showed a more gentle side to her personality when the likes of Les Kellett fought. Another hero of hers was the famous Yorkshire showjumper called Harvey Smith, a man who took on the sporting officials of the day in a unique and uncompromising way, making the two-finger gesture internationally famous! Unfortunately, it was many years later that I discovered that my father was sometimes a nervous wreck when he was a youngster still living at home; he would disappear to his bedroom, shaking and covering his ears with a pillow as his parents quarrelled and sometimes fought intensely.

Grandad died within a couple of days of me rushing back from school, making it the saddest period of my life to date, a strange thing really as I never sensed any deep affection from him when he was alive! It was the first death that I'd encountered, and the grief of losing someone so close to me seemed overwhelming at times. He was only sixty-four years old when he passed away, but he always looked much older, having previously had two strokes in his early fifties that had aged him considerably. For several nights I cried myself to sleep, pleading with God to allow Grandad into heaven, until eventually the sorrow eased and things returned back to normal again. On the day of the funeral, Nan's front room was arranged for another 'special event:' the presentation of Grandad's body, which was lying in the front room in preparation for everyone to pay their final respects. I walked past the coffin, thinking how pale and less wrinkled he looked than before he passed away, but disliking intensely what I was seeing as my stomach muscles began to cramp up. I quickly moved on through into the other room and felt more upset as each second passed by. The sadness of his death came to a head later in the day at the funeral service, when I saw the rest of my family members begin to show signs of emotion whilst Psalm 23, The Lord is my Shepherd, was being sung. As the service came to a close, family members made their way to the long black cars that were parked up outside the church and we returned to Grandma's house. A buffet meal awaited the returning crowd, and my grief became so acute as I contemplated the misery and sadness of the occasion, baffled by the idea that anyone would want to eat food at such a depressing time!

I seemed to develop a strong motherly bond with Nan Wood when she took me under her wing, and for a few years my annual holiday seemed to be left for her to arrange, with her sister, Mary. Our favoured destinations were to Saltfleet, near Mablethorpe, or Weymouth in Dorset, but the week-long holidays were supplemented with day trips to Bakewell Farmers Market and early-morning seaside trips to Cleethorpes or Skegness with my parents, hosted by the local Working Men's Club. When we headed to the south west we always travelled by coach, taking up to twelve hours to reach our destination and starting out as early as 6.00am. This was the start of a love affair with Weymouth and Portland, places that I was fortunate enough to live in when serving in the Royal Navy, at HMS Osprey, from 1981.

During the first few weeks of my naval posting, childhood memories were abundant, particularly as I walked the streets of Weymouth, reminiscing about my previous holiday breaks as a youngster. A memory dating back to 1969 stands out in particular, when I spotted a noticeable landmark that was the seafront amusement arcade, situated near the pavilion theatre. I'd ventured into the arcade in my swimming trunks, with a new friend that I'd met at our bed and breakfast accommodation, and we made our way over to the shove-a-penny machine, spotting that several coins had accumulated to the front edge of the flat surface, ready to tip into the collection ledge as prize money. It was a game that has inspired the TV show called Tipping Point, but the machine was only around six-feet wide. The temptation soon became too much for us nine year-old boys to bear, as we looked down onto the piles of copper pennies from behind the timber and glass screen. What started as a gentle nudge to the lower area of the machine soon became a real wallop with our hips, forcing the precariously balanced pennies into the collection shelf located just above our knees. Simultaneously, the beautifully coloured lights that encased the machine, went berserk, flashing in time with a loud siren after detecting our physical intrusion. Paralysed with fear, I froze to the spot as my accomplice sprinted off, leaving me to take the rap as the high-decibel siren almost deafened me. A member of staff appeared within seconds demanding that I leave the arcade immediately, with a command to never return again, and with my shame and embarrassment palpable, I never ventured back to that arcade until my posting in 1981, even after spending further holidays there!

Grandma would regularly tell me what a lovely couple my Mum and Dad were, stressing how everyone liked them, and my parents took great pride in saying that they'd never had a cross word or argument with each other throughout their married life. The statement was also verified by the way they treated me throughout childhood, kind, gentle and very patient. It was therefore upsetting to learn that Mum had a fall-out with Nan many years later, leaving it up to my sister to tell me the reason why. It seemed that Nan had been a dominating presence throughout their relationship, which Mum put up with for a long period of time, before suddenly cutting off communication and claiming that she wanted nothing else to do with her anymore. As far as I was concerned, I came from a close, loving family, so hearing this news was a real shock and I like to assume that the decision probably came about through

Mum feeling weary, after many years battling the debilitating, painful effects of osteoporosis, which had been left undetected for eight years. To add to Mum's woes, it was around this time that Nan began to suffer with dementia, but prior to her diagnosis she'd begun to do and say many offensive things. The family dealt with Nan's unusual behaviour as well as could be expected, until Mum decided to take it personally, and unfortunately they never did reconcile their differences. Because of her illness, Nan was never really aware that my mum was breaking off formal links, always asking how she was as a matter of course, when the rest of the family visited her at the local care home. How distressing this was for my dad, I'm not sure; as neither of my parents offered to speak to me about it. Not being around made me feel unqualified to give comment on most family situations; nevertheless, I felt a slight resentment towards my dad for not showing strong character to step in to sort things out, or at least having a quiet chat with me, to let me know what was going on. It was upsetting to know that Mum and Nan had got to this point without reconciliation taking place, when a discussion may have resolved the issue. We all have the capacity to let each other down, and it's something I felt when a very close friend failed to explain personally, why he'd decided to stop meeting with me on a regular basis, after doing so for many years.

As Mum and Dad's health deteriorated, Julie took on the burdensome task of becoming my parents' official carer, whilst remaining a close friend and a loving daughter, and in hindsight I am grateful for their intimate relationship. Equally so that her husband, Garry, became like a second son to them, creating a strong, close bond that was nice for me to witness whilst I lived so far away. I'd become more of a free spirit as I selfishly embraced naval life and independence to the full, having so much adventure that the excitement often overshadowed my relationship with my parents, until I came back home on leave.

Ernest and Mary, who were Mum's father and stepmum, lived on the other side of Sheffield at Norfolk Park in a first-floor council maisonette, within a block of around thirty units. I don't recall seeing much of them, although every so often we spotted Grandad as he drove a double-decker, the number 95 bus; I would wave to him, sometimes meeting him as he parked up around the corner from where we lived, at the terminus. They were a lovely couple, always well dressed, who seemed to buy everything, whether clothes or food, from Marks and Spencer, and it was always appreciated when I went to visit, staying overnight on the very rare occasion.

Christmas time at Nan and Grandad Hills was particularly pleasant, as we would be treated to what family members called a 'running buffet.' At our first 'running buffet,' I was introduced to iceberg lettuce, considered by the family as an expensive delicacy and a real favourite of Grandad's. He absolutely loved the stuff, laced with Heinz salad cream, and he never seemed too enamoured to see it being given away to other family members! Nan would spend time preparing the food in the open plan living area, before adding finishing touches to the display on the table. Then a large bowl of pale green leaves would appear, taking pride of place alongside the tinned ham and luncheon meat sandwiches, pork pie, and other basic but tasty morsels. My concept of a 'running buffet' was that we would all be asked to back off to the furthest wall, ready to start the sprint back and forth to the table with plates full of food. My childlike naivety had caught me out yet again and this amusing assumption became long-lasting in Nan's memory archives, until she succumbed to dementia in later life.

As I reached my teenage years, I was left totally perplexed at Grandad's behaviour on one occasion: he fended me off as I went to give him a greeting kiss. His character seemed to have changed as he said, "You're a young man now and men don't kiss each other." I was just twelve years old. I immediately felt embarrassed by the comment, somewhat confused, as I still gave my father a goodnight kiss up to that point. My grandparents were always nice to me, so I was deeply saddened by the rebuff and the confusion was compounded by my parents' lack of response to the situation, making me wonder what I'd done wrong. I was left to deal with the awkwardness of the moment, before sometime later Mum suggested that it was perhaps time to stop giving Dad a goodnight kiss from there on.

The same feeling of awkwardness had previously been experienced whilst on holiday at Scarborough, when I had no choice in the decision to enter the holiday camp fancy dress competition, dressed up as a 'Miss World' contestant! Mum's patience wore thin when I rebelled and protested about what was happening to me, as I was adorned with a ladies' tightly fitting swimming costume, tights, high heels and a layer of make-up and lip stick to my face. A small clump of hair was made to stand upright on the crown of my head, secured with an elastic band, whilst an elegant sash, stretching diagonally from a shoulder down to my hip, had 'MISS WORLD' written on it in dark felt tip pen. One of the two words, 'WORLD' had been crossed out, and was replaced with the word 'TAKE.' I can assure anyone, that what happened to me on that day, was definitely a 'MISS TAKE'. Being forced to appear on a raised stage in front of a large crowd, made me feel so awkward, and my levels of embarrassment reached new heights. Perhaps, it's one of the reasons that I've never felt comfortable when speaking to large groups of people.

It was my dad's habit to go for a nap every Sunday afternoon after one of his drinking sessions. I always envied this habit! Frequenting the Working Men's Club then moving on to the Hadfield pub at West Park, was a regular weekly event, before coming home and giving us a rendition of one or two classic songs, as we waited for the roast dinner to be served. I loved the fact that my parents had a big, cosy, double bed, but I was only allowed into their bedroom on Christmas morning, so I couldn't wait for the opportunity to snuggle up with Dad on the one occasion that he allowed me to come with him for a nap. I finished my lunch in record time, and changed into my pyjamas, before jumping into bed alongside him. However, as I reached over for a cuddle, Dad begrudgingly grunted, then turned over on to his side. With the back of a white cotton vest now facing me, it was only a matter of seconds before the sound of snoring was echoing around the room and my signal to ease out of the bed, and creep quietly back down the stairs. The same unease, that I'd felt from the rejection from Grandad Hill some weeks earlier, was evident again, but this time from my father and I can't recall any of my family ever hugging or lovingly embracing me; it just wasn't the done thing. Discovering 'man hugs' was a shock to the system and something I first encountered after developing close friendships at church, but the tactile activity has taken me some time getting used to, together with sharing the peace at communion. However, I realise that it is a change for the better, rather than allowing my pride or self-consciousness to dictate to me in a negative way, especially after recently losing a close friend who I will always remember for his manly 'bear hugs'.

It wasn't long into my relationship with Alison before I was introduced to her retired parents, Fred and Margaret, but it seems that they hadn't heard a great deal about me up to that time. Alison had invited her father to come and watch me play rugby in an inter-service match, against the Army at Twickenham, without actually divulging too much about our relationship. Fred was told to watch out for the Royal Navy No.8, the one with a blue shirt on, at the back of the scrum. After the game we were introduced to each other, and I assume I must have made a reasonable impression, as I was invited around to their home for Sunday lunch the next time I was in Kettering, something that became a regular occurrence thereafter. It was around three years later that another formal meeting took place with Fred, one where I asked if I could marry his beautiful daughter; the positive response made it the best thing I've ever done. As I integrated into Alison's family, I learnt that her brother, Arthur, played rugby for Barnet, whilst his full-time job was working for Barclays in the City. I recall Arthur's pride at seeing a photograph of me in Australia at Randwick Rugby Ground, famous for the Ella brothers, whilst wearing his Barnet sweatshirt that he'd kindly given to me. It was taken during one of the many training sessions during a two-week tour in 1986, to celebrate the Australian Navy's 75th anniversary.

Alison's upbringing was very different to mine, having attended a Girls' School at Retford in Nottinghamshire and achieving status as Head Girl in her final year. She later went on to university in Manchester, to study Audiology and Education of the Deaf. When we first met, she was teaching deaf children at Avondale School, Kettering, her first and only teaching appointment. Alison's promotion to Head of Unit prior to our marriage was a welcome boost to our income, particularly with the uncertainty surrounding my career prospects after leaving the forces. Our wedding ceremony took place three months after leaving the Royal Navy, on August 1st, 1987, at Rothwell Parish Church, due in part to the fact that Alison's mum was a regular attendee and it was a natural choice as neither of us were part of a church at the time. The ceremony was well-attended, with many of the children who she taught turning out with their parents to show their indisputable love and support for her. Our wedding reception was held at a beautiful hotel in Finedon, Northamptonshire and the intimate celebration consisted of just fifty people in total. It didn't go unnoticed by my naval friends that most of them hadn't received invitations. It was common to have over one-hundred people attend a naval wedding reception evening bash, so I suppose that most of my friends felt let down by not receiving an invitation. The whole day was relaxed and very family-orientated with a respectful and cordial atmosphere throughout. However, when it came to the best man's speech, I was a little nervous as he said that he was going to do an A-Z of my life. I had no idea what this meant and wasn't much bothered, as I'd changed so much since meeting Alison and I was more concerned about nerves getting to me as I thought about my own speech. Things were going well until my best man, Simon, got to the letter 'T' and said, "T is for teeth and for those of you who know Glyn, he's probably told you that he lost some playing rugby?"

I'd always told my parents that I lost my front teeth playing rugby, after a boot caught me in the mouth. The truth was that a friend and I were heavily inebriated one Saturday evening, and on our way home he produced a smoke bomb from his parked car. After much deliberation about what to do with the bomb (he'd already pulled the pin and placed it in my hand), my bottle went and I was able to transfer it back to him. Within moments, a large part of Weymouth sea front was smothered in dense, coloured smoke just across the road from where I lived, after he threw the canister towards one of the seating shelters near the King George statue. I took off as soon as he threw it but ran into a signpost head first, at great speed, which flattened me, but I instantly jolted back up from the floor, only to clatter my shoulder against the post again. As I came to my senses, I thought someone had hit me and it was only when a lad came over to help, did I realise that there was an obstacle in my way. My friend ran past me screaming with laughter, urging me to follow him, as I sprinted back to my house some thirty metres further on. The mess and damage to my face was substantial, but I couldn't get help until Monday morning for fear of being caught and blamed for the stupid act. My mum's face was a picture as the best man's shortened version of the story unfolded, with Dad sniggering throughout.

I think Alison must have loved the thought of a challenge when she took me on! When we first began dating, I would park well away from her house when I called to go out with her, implying that I'd been dropped off by a friend. I eventually owned up to being embarrassed by the condition of my vehicle, which tended to change every few weeks due to them breaking down and being scrapped. During my first season playing for Northampton Saints, they were paying me £40 to travel up from Weymouth each weekend, which meant that I needed just four trips to Kettering to cover the cost of the vehicle and all of my weekend expenses. I had a mate in Weymouth who ran a garage, and he agreed to supply me with cars for £100 that had at least three months' tax and MOT on them. But my best outlay was for AA membership, ensuring that wherever I was, whatever time of day or night, I was guaranteed a trip back home to Dorset from the Midlands, and that I would also receive up to £10 for the scrap value of the vehicle, something that became a regular occurrence.

Well before meeting Alison, my first car purchase was lavish compared to subsequent purchases, costing £200 and with a full year's MOT. Unfortunately, within seven days of passing my driving test I wrote off the Triumph Herald when I collided into the rear of a Volvo estate, whilst surveying the new styles of bikini on Weymouth sea front! But, several cars later, a Mk3 Cortina became a firm favourite. One side of the vehicle's rear suspension had collapsed over a wheel, and the gear change handle, a short stubby lever that was encased with leather, came off in my hand each time I placed it into neutral! I balanced out the rear suspension by leaving a set of training weights to one side of the boot, which counterbalanced both sides and levelled out the back end.

Alison was now very much in my life and was booked in to come and see me play against Australia in 1984, for Combined Services at Aldershot barracks. My fitness levels were below par after recently being injured, and although I was selected on the bench I managed to get onto the pitch for twenty minutes. The squad had gathered some days previously and one evening I took some teammates out for a drink in my Cortina. I pulled up at a set of traffic lights, already in high spirits and laughing uncontrollably, as my mate told the other passengers about the quirkiness of the vehicle they were in. The gear change handle was now wiggling about in my hand, when an MG Midget pulled up behind us. I stuck the handle back into first gear and held the clutch down, revving gently with the handbrake on and allowing myself a glance through the rear view mirror. The driver of the MG looked quite anxious as the street lights lit up his face in the evening darkness and as the traffic lights began to change, so I began to rev harder. Fortunately, as I released the handbrake the car stalled! I had inadvertently placed the gearstick into reverse and can only imagine what was going through the mind of the MG driver when he saw my reverse lights glaring at him as he pulled up behind me. The same car was eventually scrapped when the engine blew up on my way back from Cobham, after returning from a hotel after an inter-service match. Driving in darkness and during a heavy downpour of rain, smoke began to filter through the ventilators, making visibility poor and breathing difficult. However, my friend and I leaned our heads out of the windows and somehow limped back to base, leaving a trail of smoke behind us.

Nevertheless, Alison stuck with me and it was to be just over three years after our wedding that we started a family of our own, and Natasha Grace was born on 2nd December 1990. I'd been primed by several friends to ensure that I had lots of food prepared ready to take with me to the hospital. Their reasoning was that when a woman goes into labour, it can take hours before she gives birth. As the predicted due date passed, by several days, neither Fred, Margaret, nor I thought anything suspicious when Alison disappeared upstairs, after our meal together. It was a dark and dismal Sunday afternoon when suddenly, without warning, Alison reappeared exclaiming, "it's started." Before I knew it, we were speeding to hospital as quickly as we could, but not before I'd grabbed a small bag of Hula Hoops. Except for my hunger pangs later in the evening, the birth was as natural and pain-free as possible, for me.

It's widely accepted that if a man had to give birth, we would be extinct by now! It was excruciating to watch Alison in labour pain as each contraction weakened her slight frame more and more. It was some thirteen hours later, at around 4.00am, when Natasha Grace was born. Her little, wrinkled body appeared, slightly blue in colour indicating that there'd been complications. The maternity nurse later told us that the umbilical cord had caught itself around the baby's neck, cutting off her air supply. The midwife announced to us that the child was a girl, before gently presenting the baby, swathed in a warm towel to her exhausted but relieved mum.

My New Zealander rugby coach told me that there is no better feeling than having your first child and I wasn't disappointed with the sense of pride that I felt. My carefree daze, where nothing else seemed important other than our new family member, lasted a full ten days before the reality of day-to-day life kicked back in. All I can say is that when you commit to having children, life changes drastically, and in our case for the better.

Little did I know that I would soon be accepting that I was still a child myself, having been adopted into God's family and that my life was going to change for the better. Ephesians ch.1, v.4 says,

'For He chose us in Him before the creation of the world to be holy and blameless in his sight. In love He predestined us for adoption to sonship through Jesus Christ, in accordance with His pleasure and will.'

In May of 1991, whilst captain of Bedford rugby club, I decided to retire from the game, due to a permanent neck injury that had dogged me for the last two seasons. With the prospect of my salary being halved, as the country slipped into an economic recession, the fifty-mile round trip commute, from Kettering to Bedford was too much of an inconvenience, prompting me to leave my estate agency job for good. We had every intention to add to the family, at some time in the future, but made a calculated risk for me to set up a business, knowing that we had a guaranteed salary from Alison's teaching job to support us. We cashed in all of our insurance policies and raided our savings to reduce our mortgage to the lowest possible amount, whilst taking out a 10.2% fixed-rate mortgage over two years that was a bargain at the time. I'd had a burning desire to set up a business for a couple of years, after a friend suggested setting up our own estate agency together, but a lack of capital made me reliant on my colleague to fund the project. He decided against the idea, before we ever got to the point of discussing financing etc. so it was a bold step when Alison trusted me enough to try out a business idea, involving clearing, cleaning and maintaining the gardens to vacant properties. Such was my enthusiasm that it allowed us to forge ahead very quickly, and as the business flourished Alison was able to hand in her notice at the school where she taught, in order to look after Natasha full time, and who was now a year old. The few weeks before Alison's end of term when I looked after Natasha as a househusband didn't come naturally, creating immense respect for full-time mums, who choose to nurture their children until they're old enough to attend school.

Alison chose to embrace the challenge of motherhood and breastfed Natasha for a long period of time, as she did with Faith and Rory, and it's been both a privilege and a blessing to see parenting played out in this way, particularly as trends and circumstances have moved away from these traditional parenting roles. During those early years, a mother's work must be one of the toughest voluntary jobs in the world, where the days seem so long but the years too short. I will be forever grateful for my wife's kindness, goodness, patience and love for us all, during some very challenging times.

I've learnt that as a child you can never fully appreciate the extraordinary love that a parent has for you, until you become a parent yourself. It was therefore a further blessing when Alison gave birth to Faith Elizabeth on 1st July 1993, followed by Rory Benjamin on 9th July 1997. We've had some lovely times over the years and still enjoy spending time together, whether on holiday or visits to see each other. All three children are very different in personality, but they have always shown respect for us, for authority, their elders and are genuinely nice, loving, loyal people. I am immensely proud of them all, for just being who they are, and particularly for holding on to their Christian faith when most around them seem to challenge or deny it. They all graduated well at university, Natasha as a teacher, Faith as an architect, and Rory is currently enjoying some time abroad teaching English in Thailand and travelling, after gaining a degree in Geology.

I look back with joy, and a little envy at how content my parents were with their lot, even though they had very few material assets. However, I wonder how my sister and I might have benefited more, if my parents hadn't smoked away a big part of their hard-earned wages on cigarettes! We didn't have many family holidays, rarely ate out or had treats, but I was a happy, contented boy from a happy, contented family, and I am eternally grateful to my parents for that.

Combined Services squad v Australia, 1984. Glyn, back row, 4th from right

At Randwick rugby ground in Australia with friends Scooby and Wallace

Playing for the Royal Navy against the Australian Navy to celebrate their 75t^h anniversary in 1986

(opposite)
Our wedding day at Rothwell parish church, August 1st, 1987
(bottom left)
Alison with her parents, Fred and Margaret, and Natasha
(bottom right)
Alison with Faith, Glyn wih Natasha, 1993

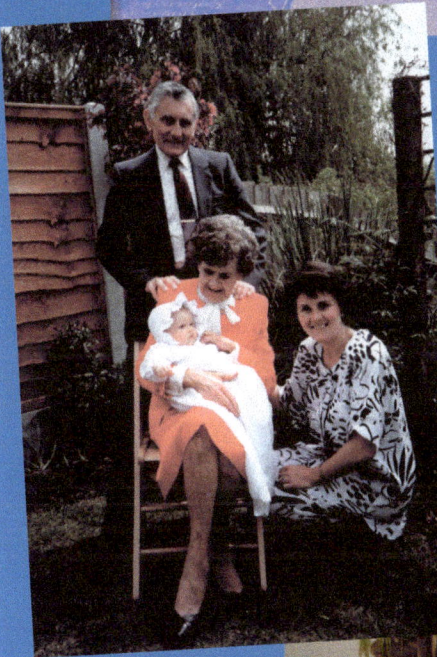

Natasha, Rory, Glyn, Faith and Alison, 2017

Grandad Hill's public transport safe driving medals

Chapter Four

BORN IN SHEFFIELD, MADE IN THE ROYAL NAVY

Without the freedom to express myself as I did in the Royal Navy, I'm convinced that the path I was following in Sheffield would have ended with disastrous consequences. I was grateful for my upbringing, but my appetite for adventure couldn't have been safely fulfilled within the confines of my family home, and it was left up to the armed forces to make me in to the person I sought to be.

My career in the Royal Navy began as a highly anticipated adventure, and ended eleven years later, aged twenty-seven, when I realised that I'd outgrown my time in the Senior Service. With a sense of excitement, mixed with fear and apprehension, I was first interviewed at the Royal Navy careers office in Sheffield City Centre, as a fifteen-year-old boy.

Dad's best friend's guidelines were etched in my memory: to be firm in my insistence that I wanted a position in the Fleet Air Arm, not the General Service. Ray was coming to the end of his naval career, after twenty two years' service, so he had plenty of experience to pass on to me, and in 1976 the General Service consisted of around 110,000 personnel, whilst the Fleet Air Arm consisted of just 10,000. I'd never had to make a firm decision about anything in my life up to this point; instead I reacted to events that were in front of me at any given time. For me to insist on something was a new and difficult concept, never mind telling a senior member of the Armed Forces that I was good enough for a career that I knew nothing about.

After receiving a warm welcome, the interview began. Why do you want to join the Royal Navy? Why the Fleet Air Arm? What mechanical experience do you have? My answers were brief but given as honestly as possible, and later, with a renewed confidence, I completed timed exams in Maths and English. By now, I knew that my school exam results were going to be disastrous but I handed in the papers, happy with how things had gone, before being paid a generous amount for my bus journey expenses. Some days later I was elated to receive a letter informing me that I'd been accepted into the Royal Navy, subject to a medical examination, so a further appointment was made with the city centre office and I was asked to bring in a urine sample. It was another opportunity to dress up in a shirt and tie, with my made-to-measure trousers and jacket, leaving our house a very smart and proud young man.

I placed the specimen bottle, full of fresh liquid, in the external chest pocket of my jacket. Realising that I was a little early for the bus I made the decision to walk the half-mile to the next stop, regularly looking back to see if there was any sign that it was on its way. During a momentary lapse of concentration, I looked up, only to see the large double-decker vehicle gliding past me, but I still had a seventy-five-yard sprint in order to join the queue, already formed at the next bus stop. As I bounded down the hill at great speed, I came to an abrupt halt, whereupon a small container of urine flew into the air from out of my blazer pocket, before smashing on the pavement floor just ahead of me. The smelly substance attracted the attention of a couple of ladies who clearly sensed my initial shock and embarrassment as I swiftly scuttled on to the bus.

The Royal Navy careers staff accepted my apologies for not bringing in a sample, asking me to provide another specimen, at a future date. I was told that there were immediate vacancies for Stewards or Seaman Trainees, but my exam passes were high enough to be accepted into the Fleet Air Arm, as an Aircraft and Engines Mechanic when vacancies arose. Further pressure was applied for me to sign up for General Service, and I was told that I may have to wait up to a year before being accepted for a position in the Fleet Air Arm. I stood firm, eventually leaving home on 24th August 1976, to join Anson 35 class as a Trainee Aircraft Mechanic. My class consisted of twenty-three other young men from various parts of the country, all following varied career paths.

We had a fantastic group, ranging from the childish sixteen-year-olds, like myself, to a more mature individual in his twenties and an eighteen-year-old who had a desire to become a commissioned officer, having previously been part of the Naval Cadets, which made him an ideal class leader. From the outset, as a collective, our class was outstanding, eventually winning Captain's Guard for the passing-out ceremony for our entry, along with numerous other accolades. Initially, I needed guidance with my kit preparation to achieve the required standard, but relished the discipline, camaraderie and teamwork that was quickly instilled in to us. It was expected that some of our kit be sprayed with starch, to achieve razor-sharp creases when ironed, and our all-leather footwear should be spit and polished, to create a mirror-like finish to the toes and heels. I enjoyed every moment of my six weeks of basic training, having a smile on my face for the full duration. I only had the odd momentary lapses when I felt slightly homesick, particularly when I received a letter from Nan Wood with a bar of Bournville chocolate enclosed – not my favourite chocolate bar, but definitely one of the more expensive at the time.

It was instilled in to us that our identity card was worth more than the crown jewels, and if we lost it, punishment would be excessive. You were expected to memorise the number so that in a robotic manner, you could repeat it at any time, something I can do to this day. Our large mess deck was on the first floor of a dull concrete building, adjacent to other similar accommodation blocks, all enclosing an inner courtyard. The living space housed twenty-four of us and had a boxed-in, vented, heating system which created a shelf around the perimeter edge of the room. My routine was to place what I needed for the following day on the shelf, ready for roll call at 6.30am. But, one evening, I tossed my identity card on the top of my pile of clothing and when I went to retrieve it, I discovered that it had slid down behind the vent where some sealant should have been. The class leader informed the duty senior rate about my predicament, who decided that It was best to leave it until the following morning to investigate further.

Within minutes of waking, our instructor appeared along with other staff, all keen to hear my version of events. The heating system was carefully dismantled and a further gap was found directly below the missing sealant, which formed the cavity to the main wall. Remarkably, my ID card had disappeared for ever. The instructor looked at me suspiciously before saying, "Wood, when this building is demolished, I shall come back to check to see if your ID card is in this wall." It was the first time he'd ever known anyone to lose their ID card during basic training.

Later in 1978, whilst training for the Field Gun at HMS Daedalus, I was worse for wear after a night out at the Bun Penny, public house. It was a venue that Field Gunners regularly frequented, within a stone's throw of our mess block but separated by barbed wire security fencing. The official way back into camp, via the main gate, was at least a twenty-minute walk, or an alternative option was to climb over the ten-foot-high fence. Within a few moments, my mind was made up and before I knew it, my friend was beckoning me from the other side of the fence. The route had been tried and tested for many years previously and was well known as being a vulnerable part of the air field boundary. Unfortunately, the alcohol caught up with me as I straddled the barbed wire, on top of the mesh fencing. I can remember singing from the fence top but nothing thereafter, until I awoke the following morning with a sore head and feeling ill. It was mid-morning before I realised that I'd lost my identity card, for a second time, and my mate reminded me that it may be by the perimeter fence. Panic-stricken, I raced over to where he said and was elated to find the card lying on the grass. It was only then that I realised how fortunate I'd been to clear such an obstacle without injuring myself.

Whistling in the Royal Navy was a sign of mutiny, dating back to the Nore and Spithead mutinies of 1797. As a cheerful teenager I'd always enjoyed whistling, but I didn't know a great deal about naval history. As we were putting on our boots in the entrance to our accommodation block, it suddenly fell silent, all except for me whistling merrily. One of the Training Petty Officers was an ex-boxer who'd taken a shine to me. He was always keen to encourage me and have lots of banter, but at the same time eager to catch me out at any opportunity. "Are you a budgie, Wood?" said the instructor. "No, Sir," was my reply. "Then why the *f**k* are you whistling? It's a sign of mutiny!" My response proved inadequate as I was made to run along the length of the corridor in front of fifty trainees, whilst flapping my arms, shouting "I am a budgie." My whistling came to an abrupt halt for many years afterwards, although it's something I find myself regularly doing now, to the amusement of my family.

It was the long-awaited moment when we had to prove what we were made of, as our class were separated off into pairs, then asked to form a square, like a boxing ring. I was paired up with Alfie, a well-educated young man with a rugby prop-like physique. We were asked to touch gloves, then fight for our lives, but instead I broke out in laughter, together with the rest of the class as he walked towards me with his face totally covered by his large boxing gloves. He realised that he couldn't see me, so dropped his guard slightly, only to be met with a gentle left-handed jab to his nose. After three further jabs, the Physical Training Instructor had seen enough. "Wood, stand over there and stop laughing."

Some moments later I was brought back to fight our eldest recruit, a twenty-one-year-old man, who stood at six feet three inches. His well-built frame towered over me, and as the call to 'box' was made, I received a thundering blow straight to my forehead, causing my legs to crumble as a spontaneous reaction to the impact. I recovered, only to receive the same treatment again, and as my legs buckled I felt my levels of aggression building up. All the lads were hysterical with laughter while the Petty Officer smirked and gave me time to recover. Little did I know that within five years I would be playing rugby for the Royal

Navy with this same Physical Training Instructor. I was asked if I was ready to carry on boxing and I was so angry that I could only nod, but Queensberry rules were now out of the window, as I swung hard at his head in blind anger. We were separated when blood began to spill from his lip, my pride now restored after the humiliation of being put on my backside, and I went on to win the Naval Air Command Heavyweight division some years later, when I fought a close friend in the Final.

The weekly disco was held in the NAAFI bar at HMS Raleigh, and most lads ventured there to catch up with each other, before dashing back to their respective mess decks. The atmosphere was always buoyant with everyone generally in good humour, and dance techniques were slightly awkward except for a few well-tutored disco and northern soul dancers. Rod Stewart's 'Sailing' was always played at the end of the evening, signalling that the disco was coming to a close. It encouraged most of us to hit the dance floor, binding our arms around each other's shoulders as we all sang the words aloud, all a bit soppy but a great track for bonding the classes together.

My mates and I left the disco one evening in high spirits and before I knew it, I found myself in an argument with a seventeen-year-old Glaswegian. The situation quickly escalated, when he first pushed his pointed finger under my chin whilst we stood facing each other. Neither of us had any intention of backing down and as the tension mounted, I felt a sudden numbness coming over me, a sure sign that I was going into fight mode. The consequences of being caught fighting during basic training would have been dire, and I was fortunate that friends from both sides intervened, although I was initially upset with them for doing so. As we walked away it was explained to me that what I thought to be the boy's finger pressing into my chin, was in fact, a metal comb. The implement had been shaped to form a point at one end, and it seemed that I'd had a narrow escape from a serious injury.

A favourite evening pastime was pillow-fighting, firstly between our own class members and as a way of honing our skills before challenging rival classes. Regular raids were then commonplace, targeting other dormitories on our floor from around 9.30pm onwards, providing they didn't get to us first. Various strikes were adopted, and a lethal favourite was to twist the pillow and case as tightly as possible before jumping up and slamming the weapon down on the top of an attacker's head, like a hammer. Unfortunately, one such blow left a young man slightly dazed and his retribution was to creep into our mess when the lights were out, whilst we all lay in bed. This would have been quite a smart move, under normal circumstances, but for the fact that he'd placed his steel toe cap boots in the pillow case, ready to inflict serious injury on me. Fortunately, he was stopped before things got out of hand, but his rage was evident for a long time afterwards.

Observing new recruits on the assault course was one of the ways that staff were able to spot who were team players or potential leaders. These were timed events, creating additional pressure to perform to our maximum. On our first outing I was the first to reach the eighteen foot high draped cargo net, which was located at the bottom of a steep bank. Enthusiastically, I leapt towards the net but my leading leg went straight through the meshed rope work, and I had no time to pull my leg back through fully, before twenty-three other recruits had begun to scale the obstacle. The added weight made the rope tighten around my ankle as I dangled upside down. I held on firmly to my leg with both hands in an attempt to stop it breaking, and I eventually became free when a few mates helped untangle me from the netting. We managed to catch up with the rest of the group without any further problems, but this sort of thoughtless enthusiasm proved to be a trait of my personality, during a large part of my time in the Royal Navy.

Further exercises involved preparing to enter a two-storey, metal-skinned building as part of a group of three, to carry out firefighting drills. Anxiety grew as a senior rate briefed us for what was expected of us. We were each given a fire extinguisher and told to remove the safety cap, once we had found the fire. This would expose a plunger, that when compressed, would release pressurised water spray through a length of thin hose. The idea was that we would carry out the exercise in darkness and we were directed to tap the back of our hand against the metal skin of the framework, in order to gauge the increasing heat and so discover the fire which was in an adjacent compartment. If the smoke got too much for us, we were instructed to get as low as possible, even crawling on our stomachs, in order to avoid inhalation of toxic fumes.

Tension was evident when two, large metal double doors opened, and the instructor yelled for our team to enter the building. It was a shock to come from bright daylight, and then be locked in a pitch-black compartment, as the doors slammed shut behind us. I panicked and immediately released the safety cap, rather than waiting until we'd reached the fire, and then blindly ran into the wall which inadvertently compressed the plunger. The extinguisher began spraying water all over me and the surrounding area, with no way of stopping the flow until it emptied its entire contents.

I knelt, and then crawled across the floor to avoid the dense black smoke, heading to the next compartment which was now glowing from where the fire was burning. We were guided into a safe position, advised to crouch behind the extinguishers for protection from the heat, then reminded how best to fight the flames. This was the moment that all three of us should have been battling the fire with a torrent of water, but barely a drip came through my hose.

My indiscretion made the senior rate shake his head in disbelief, but the lads were once again in fits of laughter as I exited the building looking like a charred piece of wood. My face and hands were black from the soot and water mix all over the walls and floor. At the time the reality of my mistake never fully registered, it was just a bit of fun that would be part of my growing up, as I got ever more used to receiving a 'rollicking'.

Another part of our training included experiencing the effects of a ship being hit by a missile, whilst at sea. We mustered at a site that included a replica of a destroyer's mess deck, which had a built in observation area to the front and where we could be observed from behind a waterproof curtain. Before entering the mess deck it was explained how best to plug various size holes, with different items like pegs of wood, mattresses and clothing to stem any flow of water. A generator pump was introduced on to the scene and then placed on the upper deck, together with ropes to lower it through a hatch if it was required. I'd already dismissed the idea of using the pump as it was far too much of a 'faff' to get it down from above. Anyway, how much water could be produced in such a confined space to warrant the use of a high-powered pump? As always, I was looking towards my class leader for instruction, inspiration and to take responsibility for my actions.

A whistle was blown, which meant that we were now in a war zone situation. The instructors gave us one last pep-talk before closing the curtain and switching on bright lights that lit up the mess deck. All twenty-four of us were wandering around like spare parts, desperately awaiting guidance from our class leader. Within a few moments' trickles of water appeared from various locations within the compartment, and timber pegs were meticulously inserted in to the weeping gaps, admired like a work of art, until the peace was broken by an excruciatingly loud noise from a claxon, a ship's alarm system used to generate an emergency response. Further commands were made over the loudspeaker system, advising us that the ship had been hit by a missile, and within seconds, gallons of high-pressure, freezing cold water sprayed us from all directions, and chaos ensued. Wooden posts, used to prop up timber beams or hold mattresses in place, were collapsing as men ran into them. Jets of water took us by surprise, knocking boys off balance, and as more and more men began to panic, it seemed that everyone had a better way of doing things than another. I found myself in the precarious position of holding one of the props upright, whilst others placed heavy wooden blocks on top to wedge the gap between it and the ceiling, whilst water gushed down my neck like a waterfall.

The water level was rising so rapidly that it soon reached knee height, just as the lighting became intermittent and the signal was given for the staff to begin throwing the first of many thunder flashes into the compartment. The noise was deafening and my immediate reaction was to release my hold on the support to cover my ears, causing it to collapse. The choice to fight, flight or freeze, found me tucked away in a corner gripping my ears with my eyes tightly shut when the lights were reinstated some moments later. We were all relieved when the water pressure eased off and promised that no further thunder flashes would be thrown, before being ordered to lower the pump down from the upper deck to commence an orderly clean-up. When the exercise was complete the instructors were quick to convey their thoughts on our relatively poor performance, part of which included my reactions, evoking a roar of laughter that lightened the mood.

Drill training intensified when self-loading rifles were introduced, and our class was selected as the 'guard of honour' at our intake's passing-out ceremony. It was fascinating to see how orchestrated our marching became in such a short space of time, as any repetitive mistakes were punished with having to run around the parade ground with the gun raised above our heads, something I only did once. We were relatively familiar with the self-loading-rifle, as it was the Royal Navy's gun of choice when it came to rifle shooting practice, a weapon that was quite easy to manage, with very little kick-back.

We were expected to learn how to shoot accurately and excitement levels rose at the firing range when we were introduced to a rapid-fire sub-machine gun, a short stumpy weapon. I enjoyed reading 'The Victor' and 'Commando' magazines as a younger boy, both guts and glory booklets telling adventurous stories from the Second World War, where the Tommy Gun and the sub-machine gun were regularly portrayed. It was therefore a dream come true, to have the opportunity to fire something similar.

After only a few minutes' training, the weapon was slung on to my shoulder by a strap, but before I'd begun firing at a target I lowered the gun to waist height and applied the safety catch. I was asked a question by the instructor and turning around to respond, the barrel was pointing straight at him, a definite no-no! The stem of the barrel was so short that it made the weapon immensely dangerous in untrained hands, as it was built to spray numerous bullets across a wide angle with very little movement required. After my indiscretion, the gun was taken off me, after several personnel were left recovering from a knee-jerk reaction to duck, and I received a severe dressing down for breaking protocol, even though I assured them that the safety catch was in place.

After just six weeks of basic training, my life had changed, bringing structure, discipline and many memorable achievements in such a short period of time. Future governments talked about introducing boot camps as a form of rehabilitation for young offenders, formulated on military-style basic training. I always considered that prison inmates would have been very fortunate to have had such good fun, rather than hardship enforced on them, but I understand that the introduction of the camps was eventually dropped, due to objections from some sectors of society.

In an ideal world it would be wonderful not to have to rely on Armed Forces of any kind, and to live in peace with everyone. I realise that dream will never happen, so my hope is that our military retains its principles of being a peace-keeping force, but that vision has, and will continue to be debated vigorously. I would support some sort of National Service being introduced, where the opportunity to be taught about budgeting, independent living, discipline, hygiene, and respect for others and self would be promoted. The opportunity to sample teamwork and close camaraderie is invaluable, when carried out for the right reasons and supervised correctly. If it were incorporated with a mixture of trade and military training over a year, with an option to prolong it for a second year, it could be an ideal training ground for employers to work hand in hand with potential employees. Young men and women would have a sense of belonging, security and structure in their lives, where they could develop life skills, build self-worth, achieve a qualification, and potentially discover their hidden talents and gifts. For many this may give them the confidence they need to pursue a work placement straight away, but for others options to pursue a trade apprenticeship, continue with a military career or go onto higher education could all be considered after a set time, whichever suited a person best. Perhaps, a commitment to help in the community or voluntary sector for a set period of time could be a further consideration! It has to be better than people being exploited, accepting cash-in-hand jobs, sitting at home or joining gangs. My hope would be, that delegation of benefit payments could then be better directed towards those most in need, with mentoring and pastoral support programmes introduced.

After completing basic training, we were split up and drafted to different camps, depending on our chosen trade. It was after completing my trade training at HMS Daedalus, in Lee-on-Solent, Hampshire that I prepared to travel home again. From a technical viewpoint it had been a difficult four months, as I wasn't mechanically minded, even having to learn the names of the most basic of tools, whilst most recruits took everything in their stride. My motivation and enthusiasm to succeed was high but my confidence low, as I considered how best to survive going forward, holding on to my original desire to play as much sport as possible and to travel far and wide.

There's no wonder that confidence in my own ability was low, as my only memory of making anything mechanical prior to joining up, was when Dad took me into the cellar at our house in Bolehill Road, and miraculously produced a second-hand Meccano set. We both seemed excited by the idea of making a crane or something similar, but within minutes the exercise had defeated both of us and the set was packed away, never to be seen again.

Family and friends were firmly on my mind, as I set off home for a couple of weeks leave, by train from Portsmouth. Still considered to be a trainee, it was regulations to travel in full naval uniform, and I was carrying a large kit bag with everything I owned, in preparation for my next draft to HMS Heron or Royal Naval Air Station, Yeovilton. The railway carriages were independent units, closed off with padded bench seats that supported baggage holders above, and access doors in between the seats that faced each other.

It was a freezing cold afternoon as darkness fell and the carriage emptied, leaving just me with a man, who was wearing a bright yellow, hand-knitted cardigan. I was trying to sleep at the time, with my legs outstretched on the opposite seat, when he appeared next to me. Not wanting to appear rude, I conversed, and then offered to share my chocolate bar with him before settling down to sleep again. What happened next started comically enough, when the man began coughing, then in unison, edged ever closer towards me. However, it soon became unnerving when I felt him touching my left hand, which was in my overcoat pocket, making my whole body go numb. In fear and to his surprise, I leapt up from my slumber, then grabbed him by the throat, pushing him effortlessly down the central aisle, screaming obscenities as I did so. I was expecting some sort of retaliation, but his response was timid, and in his denial, he asked, "What's wrong? I haven't done anything." He eventually exited at Basingstoke station a few minutes later, leaving me shaken and very nervous, particularly as I had no one to tell about what had happened. I was already keen to see my parents, but after this experience, it made me value the security of my home even more.

Returning back from leave I joined RNAS Yeovilton, the home of the Fleet Air Arm Museum in Somerset. It was here that I soon discovered the consequences of poor judgement, when I was invited to use a smuggled air pistol to shoot at a target, in one of the living quarters of the juniors' block. My aim was true, but other boys had missed the target that was pinned on a dartboard no more than four metres away, leaving splintered plaster marks all around the circular target. It wasn't too long before investigations began, leading to naval punishment for several of us, called 9s. We were instructed to muster at the guardroom several times a day, lay out our entire kit each evening, with no leave allowed during the five days of punishment. It was expected that every item of kit fit on the top of a single bed, most of which should be folded to the size of my Royal Navy Seaman's Manual, which was the size of a medium-sized hardback book. There was a slight sense of shame as I mustered each day in full view of passers-by, but at the same time it helped to integrate me as 'one of the lads', although it was a welcome reprieve to see the end of that particular week.

During an under-age drinking session in the NAFFI bar, two nineteen-year-old men shouted something derogatory, towards our group. I rarely wore my glasses out, even though my eyesight was progressively deteriorating through astigmatism, so I wasn't exactly sure who they were shouting at. However, it was an excuse for me to stand up for my friends, or add to my increasing 'macho' image, it didn't really matter much at the time. Within seconds they'd asked me outside to fight and I duly obliged, following them to a dimly lit delivery yard, to the rear of the clubhouse. Unfortunately, I was in a placid, slightly mischievous mood rather than feeling aggressive or angry, which proved to be my downfall during the fight. My friends followed me, astonished that I'd offered to take the two of them on, but what happened next served to change my cavalier attitude for the better, whilst boosting my kudos with those that knew me.

One of the pair invited me to come at him, and from that moment on, I only managed to connect with one light punch to the side of his face. The fight was so one-sided that at one point he had his knees on my shoulders, pounding my face with a clenched fist, and the thumb of his free hand served to pin down my cheek into the gravel floor. Later on, I found myself in a similar situation but this time one of my fingers was being bitten through, whilst trapped in his mouth. It was a most surreal situation as I seemed to be in a calm haze laid on my back, in a freezing cold puddle, yet day-dreaming about how best to get my magic punch in to terminate the fight. During the scrap his cowardly mate thought it would be a good idea to join in whilst I was on the ground, so began kicking at my groin and around my legs, before my friends coaxed him away. It became clear that I wouldn't back down when I continued to lunge at him each time there was a pause, and afterwards my friends told me that the fight had lasted for over five minutes, only finishing when he became exhausted from pummelling me for so long. This was a mutual agreement that left us both with a certain degree of dignity and our pride left intact, even though I got a real battering.

I walked back to the junior's block discussing the fight with my mates, somehow managing to avoid contact with the duty leading hand as we passed his office to congregate in my room, which I shared with three other boys. The swelling to my face had made me almost unrecognisable, yet I joked about it, and in that moment, I craved again for the rush that I'd just experienced. Unknowingly, both men had followed us back to our accommodation block, probably realising that they could be in serious trouble if I was questioned about my condition. They burst in on us, threatening that I would get the same again if I snitched or told anyone about the incident, clearly concerned about the consequences of their action, particularly the fact that both had joined in. I assured them that I wouldn't take it any further and as everyone left, I took a shower to calm down whilst reflecting on what had happened. I realised from the swelling to my face that I'd been irresponsible in the extreme, that I'd entered the world of street fighting, where anything went, devoid of rules or regulations. It turned out that both men were involved in hooliganism, in their respective hometowns of Hull and London, prior to them joining up and this must have been a real treat for them.

My first role, after completion of basic and trade training was with 707 squadron, a unit that maintained Wessex helicopters and supported the Royal Marines, flying them in to appropriate locations, whenever needed. It allowed me a short deployment onto a Royal Fleet Auxiliary ship called Engadine, to experience first-hand how the Merchant Navy supported squadrons during battle conditions. We saw how efficiently supplies were traded from one ship to another, how marines were effectively transported to and fro, and how well the Merchant Navy personnel were looked after, compared to us. To further deplete our morale, we learnt that the ship's staff were all paid extra money for any overtime incurred, something the men were happy to remind us of, when drinking in the bar. I was astonished to see how much better off they were compared to us, although the lifestyle would have become too mundane for me personally.

Within a few months of joining the squadron, we were all sent on a combat training exercise to Dartmoor, where the detachment set up a field site in the middle of the moors, with the intention to protect the facility from enemy infiltration over a five-day period. The opposition happened to be a Royal Marines Commando Unit, who was vastly experienced in this sort of operation. Nevertheless, we set about our business in a strategic manner, setting up a machine gun post to cover a majority of the valley below and introducing a watch system throughout the night. Observation posts were set outside the main camp for part of the night, located on the hillside where we would lay low behind mounds of earth or rocks, sometimes in freezing conditions. It was emphasised not to get too involved with the marines when they attacked, particularly if they got close enough to engage in hand-to-hand combat, as they would find any excuse to 'lamp us' (fight). I was still only sixteen, slightly apprehensive about the trip away, and not fully understanding the pitfalls of camping out in winter on the moors.

One of my first duties, within a few hours of the camp being functional, was to clear out the buckets from the portable loos, but as I lifted the lid to the first toilet the smell and sight of excrement made me heave. As was usual at the time, a senior rate told me that it was 'character building', insisting that I go back in to get the job finished. Fortunately for me, my constant retching and gagging set the rest of the cleaning crew into a similar decline, creating a lack of efficiency, and it was decided to stand me down from toilet duties thereafter whilst the others carried on.

This was serious camping, simulating war conditions, so dry clothing, proper meals and playful times were not in abundance. It was bitterly cold, so a proposal was made to only use one pair of socks and underpants for the whole week, as trying to wash and dry clothing was to prove impossible. This went against all the protocol that I'd been taught about hygiene. Although I tried not to wash my underwear, I had to accept defeat once the smell took hold. I adapted reasonably well to the grim conditions but hated the whole experience. I was therefore extremely grateful when we were eventually over run by the marines, attacking us at dawn on the last day of the exercise. A Chief Petty Officer, who towered over most of us at around six feet six inches, commandeered the only machine gun and was like a small child with his favourite teddy, when the attack commenced. He'd laid claim to it from day one, insisting that he was the only person qualified to use it during an attack. However, within a few seconds the gun jammed and a belt that housed hundreds of bullet rounds lay dormant. His booming voice ranted and raged as he attempted to resolve the blockage, oblivious to the marines who were now walking past him into our camp. The jam was cleared when the attack was well and truly over, but he insisted on firing off the remaining belt of blanks into the valley below, as we all cheered him on, whilst muttering under our breath what we really thought of him.

The month was August and the year 1979, when RNAS Yeovilton hosted an International Air Show, a time when the German Luftwaffe came over to display what was known as a 'Flying Coffin,' a jet that was renowned for accidents and was actually a Lockheed Starfighter. The hot summer day attracted a substantial audience, as I carried out minor duties to an isolated area of the airfield with several other personnel. It was around lunchtime when I heard an explosion, then saw a plume of smoke rising a short distance away. The crowd, as one, let out a fearful sigh, and fire crews suddenly went into action. The initial information was that a Starfighter pilot had managed to eject from his jet after stalling the engine, but we were later informed that he'd ejected into the ground and was killed outright, a desperately sad day for everyone involved, particularly his family, who were at the event.

During 1980 I flew out to Gibraltar to join my first ship, HMS Phoebe, a Leander-class frigate. Prior to joining the ship, I needed to experience the 'Simulator,' a mock-up of a helicopter's cockpit and cabin, which was suspended over a deep indoor pool. Our group was fully clothed in aircrew overalls, helmet and plimsolls when it was explained to us that the unit would twist and then turn during its submersion, and that we were to unclip our seatbelts once it had settled. The idea was that we should be able to escape through the emergency windows that were built into the sliding side doors, if a crash ever occurred at sea. I was positioned facing rearwards on a bench-seat that held six personnel, with just a lap belt to hold me in place. As the cabin descended, the duty divers took up their positions, having reassured us that there would always be an air pocket somewhere inside the unit, if needed. Within seconds the cabin had jolted upright, twisted and begun filling with water, and at the last moment we were instructed to take a deep breath, whilst the simulator continued its submersion, before settling upside down. Releasing my safety belt too early, I began floating upwards towards what was now the cabin floor, becoming totally disorientated and therefore unable to make my escape. This prompted a diver to grab and drag me to the safety of an air pocket, where I was given a lecture on what I'd done wrong, before making a relatively calm escape. The procedure was carried out again, but this time I was given the observer's seat, a far easier position to enable a quick getaway. However, the other guy in the pilot's seat next to me, panicked, and forgetting protocol started escaping by diving across me before the simulator had settled, catching me in the face with his elbow and foot as he did so. We all agreed that it would probably be a messy ordeal if we were ever involved in a crash at sea.

Further preparation to join my flight involved completing a mandatory two-week course in maintaining survival equipment, as well as a short introduction to understanding the dangers of nuclear, biological and chemical warfare. The sun was shining when we were made to don overalls and a gas mask, before marching for a distance, then running up a hill, making us all sweat profusely. As we came to a halt, a Petty Officer instructed us to enter a small bunker where a tear gas canister was discharged, as a way to show how effective our equipment was at protecting us against the ill effects of the chemical irritant. We then received orders to take off our masks to sample the impact the gas would have if we didn't take the necessary precautions, and my nose and eyes began running instantly. The rest of my face, neck, and throat began to react to the exposure, before being given access to water to rinse down and alleviate my discomfort. We were told that the gas was diluted by ninety percent, and if you ever want to put someone off rioting, they should be given a taste of what we had.

Our flight was transferred from HMS Phoebe to HMS Battleaxe in January 1981, before setting off on exercise for several weeks to the Mediterranean, eventually anchoring in Lisbon, Portugal. As the youngest recruit on the flight, I was given the honour of cutting the commissioning cake for our flight's inaugural visit to the ship, and it was a proud moment but I was soon brought down to earth as I settled into the cramped mess deck.

Fleet Air Arm personnel were called 'WAFUs' (meaning wet and f***g useless), whilst general servicemen were called 'Fish heads'. Banter was rife from the moment we set foot on the ship, but I gave back as good as I received and quickly made new mates on the Type 22 Frigate. The lads seemed excited by the prospect of showing me how 'general servicemen' take a 'port by storm,' as we prepared to go ashore for a bender.

A liberty boat went back and forth from the ship to the harbourside, during most of the day, and the docking station led directly to a sizeable concrete hard standing, teeming with market stalls. The vast array of fake produce on display ranged from shirts to shoes, watches to gold nuggets, and blocks of Cannabis resin were in abundance. Although sailors were rarely tempted by drugs, heavy drinking and smoking was taken for granted by a lot of my friends. A few of us started our pub-crawl, but a majority of the 'ship's company' headed straight to the red-light area, congregating at the infamous 'Texas Bar'. The venue reminded me of a small German 'Bier Keller', with plenty of 'Oompah', but there was no band to be seen, instead loud, piped music blared from several speakers located around the venue.

I manoeuvred myself away from the throng, still reasonably sober after a short pub-crawl, and sat on a table to be able to take in all the new sights. Some of the sailors were already bragging that they'd each been with several women, whilst others were being carried out, totally inebriated, ready to go back to the ship. It was a shocking sight, to see dozens of men paying to go back and forth with women of all shapes and sizes, yet intriguing at the same time. When it came to women, the thrill of the chase was always the enjoyment for me, and I didn't have any intention of paying for something that ultimately scared me.

Surveying the circus that was going on all around me, I caught a glimpse of someone pulling down the outer rim of a sombrero, whilst still in place on someone's head. The hats seemed to have been purchased in bulk by several sailors, setting a trend that was creating a great party atmosphere. The tug ripped the outer edge from its centre core, which was several inches high, leaving a Tommy Cooper-type fez, on the victim's head, with a straw halo hanging around his neck. I was utterly amused by what I'd seen, so it soon became my game of choice, until I nearly ripped someone's head off, deciding that it was best to stop playing that little game anymore. I arrived back on board after absorbing the buzz of the place, blue lights flashing, sirens sounding, with the different nationalities' 'Naval Patrols,' ensuring that their respective 'Ship's Company' got back to their ships as safely as possible. The following day, most of the men, who'd unashamedly gone with prostitutes, were acting as if this was something harmless, just like going to a fish and chip shop for a takeaway meal.

By our third night in Lisbon I was ready for a quiet evening, but my mate Tommy, convinced me that we should just have a couple of beers at the 'Texas Bar'. I agreed and, remaining sober, I enjoyed watching the antics of those around me, whilst soaking up the lively atmosphere. I began talking to some of the girls, curious to find out why they were selling themselves, but most just laughed before moving on to easier pickings, whilst one suggested that I was too nice for this place, explaining what bad people they all were and that I should get out before being tempted. After a couple of hours, I'd had enough, so began to look for my mate, happy to get back to the ship for something to eat. What I found was a burbling wreck of a man, so intoxicated that when he saw me, he quickly threw his arm around my shoulder to hold him up.

Naively, I always assumed that when friends were seemingly incapable of walking then they were extremely drunk. I learnt my lesson when some years previously, my friend 'Bull' collapsed in the NAFFI bar, after we'd had a session of under-age drinking. This nickname was given to him because his eyes bulged after the slightest intake of alcohol, reminding me of a bullfrog. He was a short, lightly built boy, who became my best mate for a couple of years, before being pensioned out of the Royal Navy after a serious accident in London. My parents and friends had taken him under their wing, to the point where he regularly came to our home on weekend leave in Sheffield sometimes without me, rather than to Stamford where his parents lived. Some years later 'Bull' had to undergo life-changing surgery involving skin grafts and weeks of rehabilitation after he fell asleep, drunk, whilst lying on his back on an underground escalator. The rotating stairs had caught his clothing and trapped him on the top stair, where it met solid ground. It still astounds me to this day that no one attempted to move him, instead people must have been jumping or tripping over his body as the metal slats slowly cut through his leather jacket, eventually shredding and burning through his skin! It was during a visit to the hospital in London that I was introduced to a patient who'd befriended him but was supplying him with cannabis, and after this visit, myself, family or friends never heard from him again.

When 'Bull' collapsed in the bar, I immediately assumed that our whole group was going to be in serious trouble, as the majority of us were under eighteen. We managed to usher him out of the building, without drawing attention to the severity of his drunkenness, then it was left to me to get him safely back to his mess. The walk back seemed to take an age as his dead weight began to take its toll. I reverted to a fireman's lift, and at the first sight of car headlights I jumped in and out of the porch fronts that were attached to the accommodation billets, to avoid the naval patrol van that toured the camp. Reaching his accommodation block, I blundered through the door of the single-storey, pre-fabricated building, waking some of the lads as I did so. All seemed concerned for his welfare, but at the same time laughing as the story unfolded and seeing how shattered I was from the ordeal. Throwing him onto his bed, compassion for my friend reached new heights when I undressed him, before gently tucking him in for the night. I was still leaning over him, ready to leave when 'Bull' opened his eyes, winked and said, 'cheers mate!' I'd been suckered and fooled but we were all in hysterics, as I tipped him out of his bed.

During our trip ashore in Lisbon, Tommy and I were politely shown out of the 'Texas Bar' by a tall and very muscular doorman, but without warning, my drunken casualty suddenly came around and began swearing at the bouncer. The doorman's fury was evident but he was unable to do anything about the situation, with so many naval security personnel in the vicinity. I tried to laugh it off, apologising to him as I grabbed hold of my mate, with the intention of removing ourselves from the dangerous predicament as quickly as possible. The foolishness of the Able Seaman knew no bounds, as he continued to display internationally recognised hand gestures to the fuming bouncer, from afar.

It was some minutes later that we were walking across 'Revolution Square,' a true historical landmark of Lisbon, adorned with flags and framed with manicured gardens. Suddenly, I heard shouting from behind and saw several men running towards us, from what I thought to be a police car. I convinced myself that the policemen wanted to chat to my friend, after having been reported by the door staff. I pleaded with him to sober up, telling him to stand up straight and to take his arm from around my neck, when I noticed that the police car was actually a taxi cab. I recognised the man at the front of the group as the doorman from the bar, before screaming at my friend to '- leg it' as I tried reasoning with the irate bouncer. Moments later, as two other men approached, the first started to swing his fists at me, furious that I'd blocked the access to his intended target. I sprinted as fast as I could ever remember, vaulting a small fence and flower border where my feet didn't touch the floor, skidding on my knees along the grass, before recovering, then sprinting off again, such was the rush of adrenalin.

A little while later, and relieved to be back on board, we began talking through the events of the night. It was explained to me, by another sailor, that he'd seen the incident, adding that the chasing group of men all had weapons, one a baseball bat, another a metal bar, and the first man a knife that he was swinging at me. I don't recall seeing any weapons, and I question the accuracy of his assessment to this day, but I didn't really let any of them get near enough to make contact with me. However, I can confirm that I never did go out for a quiet drink with that mate again.

After completing my deployment on HMS Battleaxe, I returned to Portland and joined the ground equipment section, a department located in an isolated workshop well away from the squadron's hangars. The working environment was relaxed and it was a welcome break after being sent here and there over the past year, as part of my front-line service. As I settled into a shore-based lifestyle, within twelve months there were rumblings of a disturbance with Argentina, in a place I knew very little about, called the Falklands.

An escalation of hostilities quickly developed into a full-scale war on the islands, and colleagues from my old squadron, attached to HMS Sheffield, were the first to be impacted when the ship was struck by an Exocet missile in May 1982. The ship eventually sank six days later, as she was being towed to South Georgia, and twenty people were recorded as losing their lives after the attack.

As tensions mounted, so did the bravado of some of the personnel on ground equipment section, several exclaiming how they'd wished it was them out there to fight. I was shocked to hear some of them spouting about what they would and should be doing, and made it clear that I thought they were full of rubbish. The main form of defence on a type 42 frigate was a Sea Dart missile system, and as far as we knew, the radar jamming capability of the weapon had failed miserably.

The inevitable happened and a signal was sent to our department requesting a volunteer to be dispatched immediately, to join HMS Invincible as part of the task force in the Falklands. You could have heard a pin drop as the previously loud, proud ratings, who had been boasting about what they were going to do to the 'Argies,' fell silent. Instead, the quietest junior rating on the section requested that he be given permission to sign up, and our Chief Petty Officer agreed to release him. Asked why he'd volunteered, his response was 'That's what I joined up to do, to experience a war situation and win some medals.' We all knew that if called upon, it was our job to go to war, but for this lad to volunteer, after hearing about the fate of HMS Sheffield, was remarkable.

Another mate, who was part of our wider social group, returned in one piece after the war but with a changed character. I'd recently purchased a half-share of a six-bedroom house, and bodies would to and fro from the property throughout the day and night. It was used as a meeting point to hit town, watch videos or just catch up with mates if they were passing through. None of us had been taught about or experienced shellshock; it was just a phrase we had heard and something to 'get over.' 'Scouse' told us that this was what he had, and it seemed an awfully long time before he received any help. As far as I was concerned, he didn't seem to want to snap out of it and he gradually became a loner, becoming more isolated as the weeks passed by, and I lost touch with him shortly afterwards. I now know this to be post-traumatic stress disorder, a most debilitating psychological illness, and I do hope he eventually received the right treatment and was able to make a full recovery.

During 1982 I'd been struggling with severe chest infections, so much so that the Navy rugby selectors insisted that I get checked out for TB, Pneumonia or anything else that creates infection of the lungs. The report came back with nothing of any consequence, other than to take antibiotics for the problem. I was now playing my club rugby for US Portsmouth and representative rugby for Hampshire, Royal Navy and Combined Services, but the heavy build-up of mucus was undoubtedly hindering my fitness.

My persistence resulted in another medical examination taking place, with a diagnosis of having blocked nasal passages, a consequence of regular impact damage causing the nasal septum or cartilage to distort. I was immediately booked in to have surgery at the Naval Hospital Haslar, Portsmouth with orders not to play rugby for at least three months. However, I took the decision to have a run-out for the camp side at Portland, after just four weeks, to retain some match fitness, but my time on the pitch was short-lived. A ruck had formed when I bound onto our open side flanker from five metres out, ready to drive into the group of bodies that had formed over the ball, when he abruptly stopped dead at the point of contact. With no time to protect myself, my face crashed into the top of an opponent's head causing further damage to my nose and putting my recovery back by several weeks. Asked why he'd bottled out of hitting the ruck, my mate said, "There's no f***g way I was driving in there at that speed!"

Yet again, injuries were having an impact on my fitness levels, but my disappointment was short-lived, when I was asked if I'd like to participate in Bobsleighing. Arrangements were quickly made for me to have time off, and I soon found myself travelling as part of a team of four, representing the Royal Navy to compete in several competitions around Europe.

It was a rugby colleague, called Bob, who first approached me to be his brakeman and I was introduced to Ginge and Topsey, when we went to practice at Thorpe Park, Surrey. The British Bobsleigh Association had a concrete base constructed, that accepted a two-man sled with wheels to be inserted into a metal track, allowing competitors to practice starting technique and to sprint down a slope for a few metres. We just needed 'Eddie the Eagle' to turn up and start jumping off a box to complement us, but this was all well before his time. Ginge made it clear that he and Topsy were the No.1 team for the Royal Navy and Bob and I No.2 team. However, after our first few competitive runs in the two-man sled at Igls in Innsbruck, Bob and I produced faster times and rankings should have been revised. Bob lacked experience in driving four-man sleds, and when the time came it was left up to me to push the other three team members, with Ginge as driver.

Bob and I were considered to be novice's, but I was giving my 'hefty' driver exceptionally good start times, particularly as he was jumping in the sled very early, which slowed us down, and it hadn't gone unnoticed by some of the Great Britain crew members. As our start times got quicker the dangers of the sport became more apparent, and whilst in Winterberg, Germany we had two bad crashes within three days. Our first mishap occurred in a four-man bob halfway down the track at 60mph, and the other in a two-man sled. My diary explains that I was badly knocked about after a terrifying ordeal in the two-man bobsleigh, tipping over at bend five, and travelling approximately three-quarters of a mile, regularly spinning 360 degrees as our speed exceeded 60mph. At the time, I was treated for just a badly bruised shoulder, but it was whilst running in Koenigsee, two weeks later, that the incident caught up with me. Throbbing headaches suddenly became a nuisance, before I was taken to hospital for a check-up and diagnosed with a bruised brain. At the same time, my driver was hospitalised for a severe infection to a damaged knee, the belated after-effects of the same crash. Although Bob and I were badly shaken immediately after the crash, the toughest part of the ordeal was getting in the sled straight afterwards and completing another run. This is strongly advised in order to regain confidence as soon as possible.

We travelled around the continent, participating in organised tournaments against a mix of international and novice teams, progressing and building in confidence as we did so. Our touring vehicle was an antiquated lorry, like a World War Two army transporter, with a canvas top. As two of us camped in the back, the other two would occupy the cabin, driving as hard as possible but struggling to reach 50mph with our double-decker trailer attached. We were carrying two, two-man bobs and one four-man bob when we travelled, and during a trip on an autobahn whilst my driver and I relaxed in the back, we picked up speed on a downhill stretch. The inhalation of diesel fumes was always a concern to our health, but to hear a crack, bang, then wallop, was a sign that the rattling engine had eventually blown up, or so we thought. The vehicle slowed as the driver hit the brakes and began to manoeuvre from the middle lane, just as the heavy-duty trailer overtook us on the outside before swerving across the front of the vehicle and slamming in to crash barriers, bringing it to a shuddering halt. How we rescued the kit or made it to a garage, I can't recall, but it was a relief to know it wasn't the engine that had blown up, and just a cracked welded joint that had snapped.

However, I was elated when arriving in St Moritz sometime later, to be asked by the current Great Britain No.2 driver if I would push him, and it was an opportunity that I grabbed with both hands. After the first run the driver revealed that it was the fastest start time he'd ever had, and that he wanted me as his brakeman from now on, tempting me with the offer to participate in the World Cup in Lake Placid and the Olympics in Sarajevo the following year. Disappointingly, neither honour came about after the driver was told by his superior officer, an Army Major and GB selector, that his hopes for promotion or a place in the GB team were nil if he chose anyone other than a soldier to be his brakeman. I'd already cut short my trip with the Navy team and returned home to get further time off, when the bad news was sprung on me. Politics had intervened and I was helpless to do anything about it, but, embarrassingly, reports of my endeavours had already been put in print by Naval hierarchy, making the missed opportunity even more difficult to accept.

Sometime later, in 1985, I was assigned to the flight of HMS York when we found ourselves in the Bay of Biscay, notorious for rough and inclement weather conditions. Whenever possible I was now travelling to Kettering at weekends to see Alison, and play rugby for Northampton

Saints. However, during this particular season, I never knew whether I was in the first or the 2nd XV, until I could get to a telephone to ring her, after she'd previously been notified on my behalf. The club would send out a postcard to let you know the details of where, when, and who you were playing for, which all added to the excitement of representing a senior club.

The ship was due to dock in Devonport by Friday afternoon, but we first had to negotiate force eight gales with wave swell as high as thirty feet. The hatches were closed down and personnel were asked to stay in their mess deck, unless on duty. To combat sea-sickness, it was preferable to locate to the rear or stern of the small destroyer, a great advantage for the flight members as the hangar and deck were positioned there. We took up our relaxing positions on inflatable liferafts, stored upon the mezzanine balcony that surrounded parts of the helicopter hangar, knowing that the upper deck was now totally out of bounds. Nature eventually called but the thought of opening and closing several metal hatches to get to the communal latrines was too much to contemplate.

Instead, two of us opened the side door that gave access to the sidewalk and flight deck, when the gale force wind took charge of it, slamming it open. I stepped out over the threshold and before my foot had touched the deck, my glasses were whipped off my face, never to be seen again. Nevertheless, I completed the task of using the flight deck as a toilet, after all, we were always taught to improvise. So strong was the wind and so volatile the sea, that the 'sea dart' missile launcher, bolted to the bow of the ship, had been severely twisted and was strapped down to prevent it from being ripped from its mountings. Our speed was no more than two knots, as the Captain negotiated the torrid conditions and allowed each one of us a call home. I contacted Alison to let her know that I would be docking a day later than anticipated, with no opportunity of making it to Kettering and to notify Northampton about my situation.

Overall, I was deployed to three front-line ships – HMS Phoebe, HMS Battleaxe and HMS York – serving only three months at sea during my eleven-year career and taking in trips to Scandinavia and the Mediterranean. I fulfilled my ambition of playing lots of sport but aspirations to see the world were less so, although rugby tours to Australia, Berlin and a couple of months touring around Europe whilst bobsleighing were most enjoyable.

During my last year of service, I was handed the responsibility to look after the Ground Equipment for 815 squadron. This was one of Prince Andrew's workplaces when he was a pilot on Lynx helicopters, but I only ever saw him once. The ground equipment section sprawled over a large part of the hangar, the equipment having been badly maintained or robbed of vital components by flights, as they deployed to their ships. I was allowed autonomy to rectify the problems on the section and went about creating a culture of accountability, which wound up many senior rates. Assisted by some friends from other departments, I was able to restore much of the stock, creating a system worthy of me gaining recognition in the form of a prestigious Admiral's award for proficiency. Yet again I was able to show that given the opportunity, in the right environment, I was more than capable of achieving worthwhile results. I left the Royal Navy in 1987, with no regrets knowing that it was the right time to go.

The Royal Navy employed me for ten years and nine months from the age of sixteen years and three months old, paying me a reasonable salary to share my time between being an Aircraft Mechanic and as a sportsman. I participated in many activities to a good standard, including rugby, athletics, field gun, boxing and bobsleighing, but with the exception of boxing all the other sports were fully amateur at the time, and I felt privileged for being paid to actively participate in them. I was quickly recognised as a sportsman who had potential, forever grateful for the opportunity to take part in so many different recreational activities, but I also think they got good, committed, entertainment out of me. The fitter I got, the more I seemed to excel at any sport that I cared to try and although rugby union remained my preferred sport, risking life and limb doing other activities seemed to suit my temperament.

Anson 35 class, HMS Raleigh. Glyn, front row, first left

New recruits, Mick and Glyn at HMS Raleigh training base, Torpoint, August 1976

Guard of Honour, HMS Raleigh passing out ceremony, October 1976. Glyn, front row, first on the right

My first front-line posting on the flight of HMS Phoebe

Royal Navy squad at Twickenham, 1983
Glyn, back row, eighth from the right

Bobsleighing; brakeman at St Morritz, Switzerland, shortly after
crashing twice at Winterberg, Germany

Cutting the flight commissioning cake on HMS Battleaxe

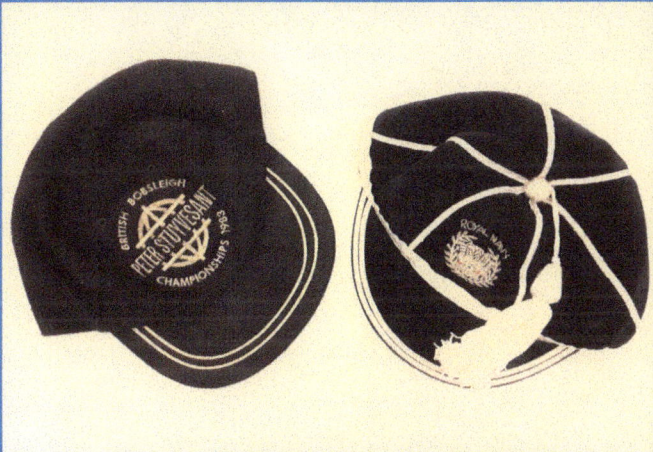

My British Bobsleigh Campionships cap
and Royal Navy cap

On my way to winning the Fleet Air Arm Heavyweight boxing final

Chapter Five

THE TOUGHEST SPORT IN THE WORLD?

I didn't know it but in 1978 a documentary was being made by the BBC called *To the Limit and Beyond*, in which a seasoned commentator, Ian Wooldridge, proclaimed that Field Gun was the "toughest sport in the world". From an early age it was made clear to me that showing emotion was a sign of weakness, so after moving away from home it was imperative that I toughened up quickly. Playing rugby with adults from the age of sixteen, whilst also competing in the Fleet Air Arm Field Gun Crew at the Royal Tournament in 1978 as an eighteen-year-old, was all part of my initiation process.

I was the second-youngest person to ever represent any of the Field Gun crews at Earls Court throughout The Fleet Air Arm, Portsmouth or Devonport, and as part of my induction to this unique sport, I'd previously participated in a mild version of Field Gun, called 'Brickwoods', something that is still in existence to this day. The 'Brickwoods' competition was an annual event held at HMS Collingwood, between numerous naval establishments on a flat, tarmac track, with no obstacles to negotiate. A gun and limber are dismantled and shells fired at various points along the track, all carried out at high speed. In 1977, as a representative of HMS Heron or RNAS Yeovilton, we finished as victors of the competition, giving me an insight into how fit I needed to be for the real Field Gun Tournament held at Earl's Court.

For such a minor event, I found the intensity of the training for 'Brickwoods' very demanding, as we were expected to meet as a squad three times each day to participate in organised exercise, starting at 6.30am, again at lunchtime, then as soon after 4.30pm as possible, when our daytime work was finished. I was selected to run my position ahead of an ex-Devonport Field Gunner, who was also a Royal Navy athletics sprinter. Such was my confidence in my own sporting ability, that I thought nothing of my accomplishment, remaining modest rather than proud, even though I received many plaudits from those involved with the sport. It was to be a long time before I began to understand how the ex-Devonport Field Gunner must have felt at being overlooked, and a young sixteen-year-old boy taking his place, but I remember how humble he was with the decision. I have no doubt that most sprinters would have beaten me over anything more than a forty-metre race, but as constantly proved over the next decade, I had a powerful turn of pace that stayed with me as I grew in height and weight. It was a wonderful gift that suited the many team sports that I engaged in.

The origin of the Field Gun competition was to pay homage to the men who hauled the heavy artillery, across ravines and rough terrain during the Boer War in South Africa. In 1899, large field guns were landed by the Royal Navy from HMS Terrible and Powerful, before being transported by oxen and naval personnel to support the British Army, which was under siege at their garrison at Ladysmith.

The sport is held in high esteem throughout the Royal Navy, with many a reputation ruined or made, depending on how the participants fared, if they ever found the courage to attempt the selection process. The initial fitness conditioning that preceded the actual training with the equipment was intense and was meant to break you. I first joined the Fleet Air Arm training camp as a seventeen-year-old boy, in January 1978 at HMS Daedalus and I weighed in at around thirteen stones. I was astounded to see that my body was showing the benefits of the gruelling fitness regime, in a very short period of time, and I was now being tipped to be the next Navy rugby winger, athletics sprinter, heavyweight boxer or anything else other people wished to fantasise about. What was conclusive was that by May of the same year, I was selected as the 'A-Crew' Flying Angel, my weight now settled at around fifteen stones.

When I was sixteen I'd had experience of how tough the training would be, whilst qualifying as an Aircraft Mechanic at HMS Daedalus, when my friend and I chose to attend the camp trials. We shouldn't have been allowed to join in, as there was no possibility of new recruits ever making the team for that year. However, by the time the Field Gun staff had registered what was going on, combined with our enthusiasm for the challenge ahead, we were allowed to continue. The staff were astonished at my resilience, particularly after discovering that I'd completed a cross-country run four hours earlier. But my youthful enthusiasm dwindled somewhat when I realised that the twenty-minutes workout was just the warm-up before the real endurance test began.

I was already in a bit of a daze as I gasped and began heaving, then coughing up bile, just ten minutes in to the circuit-training. My lack of experience in pacing myself was now taking its toll, but my ability to recover and keep going was a natural part of my make-up and something that shone through at the trials. I was told that it wasn't possible for me to go forward for selection for the team for that year, only because I was too inexperienced in my chosen career path as an Aircraft Mechanic. However, as my draft to Yeovilton was confirmed, the Physical Trainers and senior members of the rugby team encouraged me to prepare for the following year, when I should have been well versed in naval routine.

A year later I was fortunate enough to get through the trials, and I was posted back to Lee-On-Solent to begin training in earnest. The process to build you into the machine they required, was tough at best but cruel at times, beginning as early as 6.30am with a 'wakey, wakey' jog to the main gym and back, located at the other side of the camp, and finishing each day after strenuous workouts in the morning and afternoon. Weekly elimination tests were quickly introduced and we were told to eat as much as we could, train as hard as possible, and ensure that we pushed ourselves to the limit in everything we did, because we were being 'watched'.

There was no science involved in our development, no balanced diet or nutritional surveys carried out; in fact, there was a genuine lack of knowledge about such things. 'Show some dog' was a regular cry from the staff, particularly as we neared exhaustion. Perhaps, a better interpretation of the term would be to say 'stop whinging and push through the pain barrier', there was certainly very little sympathy shown to anyone. Prior to this time, I assumed that a sign of being fit meant that I should never feel uncomfortable or breathless, even after a 'beasting'. I was therefore always left slightly disappointed with my performance, as I constantly felt uncomfortable and breathless. My misinformed view therefore shaped my character into someone who would always push harder and never give up, as I strived to discover my limitations without feeling exhausted. It wasn't until a friend offered me some basic advice, that I began to better understand my body, and it taught me how to pace myself better. He explained that I will always feel some discomfort, particularly when being pushed to achieve higher levels of fitness, but it's how fast you recover that indicates how fit you've become.

To digress for a moment…Aged fifty-five, I decided that I would try a new sport of sailing, something from past experience I knew I had little passion for. Nevertheless, I signed up with a local club at Cransley reservoir, with a desire to push through the three-day course, anticipating that I still had the determination to fulfil something that required a good level of physical and mental perseverance. The event quickly became a real challenge for a host of reasons, culminating in me leaving on day three.

I was struggling to coordinate wind and sail conditions, feeling pain from old rugby related neck, wrist and back injuries, and suffering from a stomach upset, during most of the second evening. I attended the third day, knowing that it was to be the first time in my life that I'd ever started a challenge of my choosing and would be pulling out before completing the task. The decision was made harder by the fact that I knew the instructors, who were aware of some of my past sporting exploits. Far from feeling a failure, as I would have done in my younger years, there was a realisation that I was now in a season of exploring and it felt good to be able to make decisions of my own, without having to justify my reasoning or match other people's expectations of me. I knew that I wouldn't want to regularly sail again, so arrived on the last day with mixed emotions, but happy enough to say thanks, but no thanks.

It's a beautiful gift to have freedom of choice, one that I thank God for each day. I've since tried golf and snow-boarding, but both sports aggravated my neck and hips and I've now decided that I'm best suited to walking. A trek in 2017 to Base Camp, Mt Everest, was a great adventure and test of endurance that I valued for many reasons, none more so than being able to accomplish it with my son Rory, who was then twenty, alongside me. The downside of this experience was suffering with altitude sickness, followed by a bout of depression when I returned back to England. Thankfully these worrying symptoms only lasted for two weeks.

Back to the Field Gun Training...As our limits of physical endurance were pushed ever harder; the weekly eliminations grew more intense. A typical elimination day would start with circuit training and grid sprints in the morning, followed in the afternoon by a run over five miles, where we were expected to beat our previous time over the same route. Sometimes the gruelling test would be carried out wearing steel toe-capped boots, other times carrying a sand bag, or both. The last mile was raced on a part of the Solent's shingle beach, where solid timber breakwater barriers served as hurdles. To rub salt in to the wound, a staff member would cycle along the seafront pathway, barking orders at us to run quicker or to push ourselves harder, as a form of encouragement to catch up the guy in front.

At other times we would be taken by lorry into the countryside, split into teams of eight, before being presented with logs weighing one-hundred-and-twenty pounds, which had eight rope handles fixed to them, four to each side of the beam. We would then run with the logs until told to stop, and then carry out exercises without the timber pole ever touching the floor. Difficulties occurred for the taller men when we were asked to transfer the log from waist height to shoulder height, creating a real imbalance as the beam hovered over some mens' shoulders. I was always bemused to hear the smaller guys' cries of pain as they seemed to be holding onto the log rather than supporting it, forcing additional weight down on to the taller guys' necks or shoulders. Another nuisance was, as soon as anyone got out of step the log would begin to bounce up and down, or inexplicably, from side to side, making it awkward to maintain a cohesive running rhythm.

Exaggerated facial expressions together with lots of grunting were common by some, used as a way to try to convince staff that they were really trying hard. However, the staff were wise to the fact, leading to any offenders having to carry out extra amounts of press-ups, burpees, or squat thrusts, when caught out. On our final elimination test in 1981 we were pushed to our limit, and as we approached the lorry, that was to be our transport back to camp, the vehicle drove off. We were then ordered to continue running with the logs. Fortunately, the lorry had parked up only a few hundred metres away, but was hidden by the dense foliage of the woodland so that we had no idea how much further they wanted to push us.

From around two-hundred-and-fifty candidates, forty were selected to form the A and B crews, each consisting of eighteen men with four additional guys who were nicknamed 'Tits In,' an unfortunate title implying that they were only there to do the washing up, with their 'Tits In' the sink. What better incentive to try harder than the rest to rid yourself of such a slur, but few ever succeeded, other than when injuries dictated a change of personnel. We all lived together in one large mess deck, with a separate galley kitchen and dining area, an attached shower block, and a weight training gym completing the facilities. Most of the men enjoyed going out for a few beers each evening as a way to wind down, but except for weekends, eating was always more of a lure for me.

However, it was expected, under-age or not, that we would all have a blow-out on Saturday evenings, as a way of bonding together after a strenuous week. Our final practice run would be at lunchtime on

Saturday around noon, after which some men would go home to their families whilst the remaining members generally went shopping. It was on one such trip in 1978 and after returning from Portsmouth, that I decided to lay on the top of my bed, before going out in the evening. My prize purchase from the shopping trip was a family box of Smarties that I'd carefully hidden under my bed on the floor, out of site from predators.

I awoke, instantly relishing the thought of how fast I could devour the sweets, pondering whether I should pour them straight into my mouth, or cup them in my hand before hoovering them up like a vacuum cleaner. Still in a dreamlike daze, I flopped one arm over the side of the bed but as I located the box, I sensed that the outer plastic covering had been removed and I knew instantly who the culprit was likely to be. Jock was a legendary procurer of anything that had not been securely chained down, food or otherwise, and I'd already seen him replace his worn-out 'Desert Shoes' when he acquired another pair from an intoxicated individual, at a recent party.

My disappointment soon turned to joy as I heard the chocolates rattling in the cardboard container, so relieved that he'd not eaten them all. I therefore made the decision to pour the sweets into my hand, only to discover that he'd replaced them with pieces of shingle. I could only laugh aloud as sand and gravel tipped into my palm, later complimenting Jock on his patience, ingenuity and effort after he'd gone to such trouble to fool me. This was a trait of naval humour that was prevalent in my friendship circles, particularly when food was left unattended and something, after being taught by the master, I became adept at dishing out.

A 'run' consisted of three parts: the 'run out,' 'run back' and the 'run home.' Each component was timed, then the three elements collated after penalties were added for any indiscretions. An overall time could then be announced for the complete run. Every season the three commands of the Fleet Air Arm, Devonport and Portsmouth would all try to be the first crew to register a 'clean run' under the psychological barrier of three minutes, something that seems impossible when you first start using the heavy gear. To be the first to claim the prestige of cracking the three-minute barrier could affect opposition morale, a real statement of intent, which said we were ahead of the game in preparation to meet you at Earl's Court. However, I don't think I could ever say that I was confident about achieving anything special in 1978. The monotony of the physical training, accompanied by the savaging we endured on the track, slowly took its toll physically and psychologically on all of us. It was accepted that injuries were part and parcel of the game, and something Ian Wooldridge often referred to in *To the Limit and Beyond*.

My position was generally delegated to a lighter person, but this year they experimented with me, a six-feet two-inch heavyweight, currently playing my rugby on the wing and representing the Royal Navy and Combined Services at under-19 level. I'd initially been pencilled in for the No.17 position, but at the last moment I was delegated the No.9 role, a decision that seemed to be a gamble, but it eventually turned out to be a good choice. However, I certainly didn't think so initially, as within a couple of weeks of training with the equipment I'd received permanent damage to my hand.

On the run out, I helped to erect the rig on which the cables were supported, and then returned the fifty-pound traveller at high speed, until all the personnel and the many parts of the gun and limber had been hauled across the chasm. Unfortunately, from time to time, some of the crew were caught out by the speed of the returning traveller, resulting in head and facial injuries. I would then haul myself across the chasm, chasing after the limber ready to take up my position alongside one of the wheels, as three shells were fired that signalled completion of the run out.

On the run back, a team of us lifted the limber over the wall before vaulting it. I would then sprint ahead, ready to commence with the traveller returns. Once all the team members and kit had reached the opposite side of the chasm, the metal cable would be slackened and that was my cue to unclip it from the top of a ten-foot pole. I then dropped from a standing position to do the splits on the top of the ramp, with the weight of a sixty-five pound piece of timber being absorbed by my hip. If all went smoothly, the dive onto the returning traveller, known as the 'Flying Angel', was well coordinated and I would be hauled over to the opposite side of the chasm. The rig would collapse all around me and I would take up my position by the gun, as a further three shells were fired.

The run home was executed after all parts of the gun and limber had been fed through a small partition in the wall, before being fitted back together again, then hauled as quickly as possible over the finish line.

An annual pilgrimage occurred each year, where the Field Gun Crew would attend Twickenham to watch the Army play the Navy at rugby, in the inter-services competition. It was on one such occasion in March 1978 that my friend 'Wally,' the same lad who'd come with me to the Field Gun trials as a sixteen-year-old boy, was a little overzealous in his adoration of the Navy team. It was permissible to drink alcohol in the stands and use implements like wooden rattles to make excruciating noises in support of your team. The crew's 'chippy' took it upon himself to make a very large, wooden rattle that would have scared any pigeons off for miles around, and a drunken Wally eventually assumed responsibility for the weapon. Swinging the instrument around his head with both hands, singing to his heart's content, was a sight to behold, but as his actions became more erratic, he knocked himself out, cutting his eyebrow badly in the process. As he lay slumped on the floor, someone picked up the weapon of mass destruction and continued irritating everyone with it again, whilst Wally was refreshed with yet another beer as the Field Gun doc stitched him up.

Being in stitches took on a whole new meaning many years later, when one of the Kettering members took a tumble in the rugby clubhouse. Most of us heard the commotion, but very few saw the flight-and-crash landing as he fell head first down the timber staircase that separated the first-floor bar area, from the ground-floor changing rooms. As his best friend, a practising GP, staggered to his aid, the rest of us left them to sort out the trauma, after realising that the blood spillage was inconsequential. He received a cut just above an eye, quite deep and over an inch long, which the doc began to stitch. Several onlookers gave running commentary on proceedings, as they hung over the timber landing partition that offered a grandstand view as both friends sang merrily on the steps of the staircase. The pair eventually returned to the bar in fine spirits, but on closer inspection, the gash was still seen to be gaping, with the needlework achieving a reasonable score of five out of ten, but an inch above the intended target. The sight was enough to put me off eating.... but only for a few minutes.

Between January and April in 1978, over two-hundred disappointed men were sent back to their original Air Stations, including Wally. The rest of us were now practising drills with the equipment and expected to complete eight full runs a day, once we got the hang of things. To achieve this quota sometimes meant starting a run up to fifteen times a day, but our record for this year was twenty-one starts in one day and by 7.30pm of that evening the first trainer walked off, disgusted with our efforts. I was concerned about the injuries that I was accumulating, as within a few weeks I'd lost several finger nails and most of the fingers on my right-hand had been stitched. The metal wheels and handle on the traveller were clipping my hand as I dived onto it, carrying out the drill for the 'Flying Angel', and the index finger had become so vulnerable, that it appeared to be a mass of cream and pink pulp hanging on to the end of my top knuckle. Further damage was inflicted to my right knee and an additional nuisance was that I'd gained several deep lacerations to my groin, as the wheels of the traveller cut through my trousers into my skin.

I can't recall much intervention from the staff to help stop the damage, and it was only when the medic let it be known to the first trainer that I could lose a finger, that decisive action was taken to help me. I obtained some protection by wearing a fine leather aircrew glove on my right hand, with a metal splint taped over the top of my index finger. Layers of padding were inlaid to the inside of my trousers, which cushioned the blows to my knee and stopped the cuts to my groin. Thankfully, as the season progressed my confidence stabilised, but I realised that I wouldn't wish this punishment on my worst enemy. The pride of wearing the tracksuit, even performing at a prestigious military tattoo where I was televised kneeling in front of the Queen, didn't matter anymore. I was so emotionally drained by the time we were competing at Earl's Court, that I found the pressure of running in front of large crowds quite daunting. I was now desperate to speak to my family, but only Nan and Grandad Hill had a telephone. Nevertheless, I rang them expecting that they would sense that I was in need of reassurance or an encouraging pep talk. The conversation barely got past the 'how are you, what is it you're doing' etc., before Nan said that she'd see me soon when I got home, and I placed the payphone back down on the receiver, feeling like a lonely boy, all by himself, in a man's world. As we travelled up to Earl's Court, we were invited on a trip to the Guinness Park Lane Brewery, where we were guests of honour, enjoying a silver service meal with drinks. The occasion was a memorable one, although it did little to uplift my morale, but it was a nice gesture, never to be repeated.

Getting through the season without serious injury was an achievement in itself, but it was helped when a decision was made for me to refrain from practice runs at Earl's Court, after I took another severe knock to my index finger during a practice run. For weeks I'd been mindful of the medics' observation that further damage to my finger would lead to amputation. Believing that the decision was now a reality, after seeing blood seeping through my splint, my emotions got the better of me after feeling that I'd let everyone down. The doc's assessment was that the metal splint had protected my finger adequately to not warrant surgery, which was a relief, and I couldn't wait for our time at Earl's Court to come to an end. After such a torrid experience, I was feeling that there was no way I was going to compete in the Field Gun Competition again. As a team with numerous injuries and morale at an all-time low, we stood no chance of competing, never mind winning the tournament.

The worst injury that I saw was when one of the 'B Crew' gun numbers pushed the full weight of the barrel end, weighing nine-hundred-pounds, down on to his steel toe-cap of a boot. I was watching from the stand as the heavy end of the barrel appeared on top of the wall on the run back. Unfortunately, for Nick, as the lighter end of the barrel was being forced into the ground, it hit his boot, denting the steel toe-cap into his foot like a guillotine. All I saw was his head bobbing up and down, before he collapsed with the pain. The screeching was deafening but we all thought he was just being over dramatic, as was his norm. Fortunately, the track was made up of fine compact shale, rather than concrete or similar, allowing his boot to become embedded in the surface, albeit trapped by the downward pressure of the barrel as it bore down on his toes. Without doubt, this saved his toes from being severed but as the barrel was carefully eased away, his boot began leaking blood. Nick was taken to hospital but failed to recover in time to run again, and after returning from hospital with his foot in a plaster cast, he was assigned to the sink where he spent the rest of the season as a 'Tit's In'.

My perception of this particular year was that there was too much emphasis on testing how tough we were rather than how fit they could make us. The added monotony of the training schedule made the whole experience more akin to being punished, rather than being trained to physical perfection. Some of the staff seemed to thrive on seeing us underachieve, almost like they'd given up on us, and I recall disliking some of them for their arrogance. However, I got to like them as the years passed by, but I am still left wondering if man will ever accept or understand the difference between the attractiveness of being 'masculine,' rather than the ugliness of being 'macho'?

Whilst I didn't realise it at the time, I'd actually set new standards throughout the Fleet Air Arm, Portsmouth and Devonport commands, in the way that I was able to speed up the traveller returns. I accept that I was too heavy to fulfil the 'Flying Angel' drill, in an elegant manner, but I'd discovered a new technique to return the traveller that enabled us to make up lost time or even charge ahead. I was therefore chased to return again three years later when it was explained to me that things had moved on, for the better. I was promised that the training was to be far more varied, with damage limitation a priority. Things had to change, and after our debacle in 1978, it seemed that the sport underwent a transition for the better.

In Field Gun it was particularly difficult to represent your team on multiple occasions, due to the many stipulations imposed on individuals who chose to return. You could only re-apply to join every three years, but once you'd represented any crew there were only twelve ex-members allowed to represent any future forty-man squad. A good friend from my early days in the forces, managed to make the A crew on seven separate occasions, an incredible achievement and probably a record that's never been matched. The tournament was a prestigious event, with the opportunity to perform in front of the Royal Family, enjoy substantial food rations, and the added bonus of a relaxation of some naval regulations. Judging by further positive changes that took place during the interceding years, I was therefore convinced by what my new trainer told me, so I returned in 1981 and then again in 1984, with renewed confidence. My time under both trainers was a far more enjoyable, fulfilling experience, and our performance reflected that in both years, although our results were better in 1984 when we were close to breaking the record for the fastest-ever run. It was third time lucky, when we finished as joint-winners with Portsmouth at the end of the tournament.

My 21st birthday was commemorated during the 1981 season and after celebrating my 18th birthday at the same place three years earlier, I was left wondering when my special cake might appear! Instead, the crew captain, Don, a close friend who I lived with for a while, ordered the rest of the crew to hunt me down. I managed to evade them for several minutes but eventually agreed to receive my birthday punishment, whatever that entailed. On a hot, sunny day, I was tied down on one of the ramps, hands and feet splayed apart like a star shape, and the day's slops (waste food) was brought out in a dustbin and poured over me. Left alone to bake for a while, I was then released and normal birthday celebrations commenced, but not before rushing to the showers to clean up.

After this season, six of us flew off to San Antonio, Ibiza for a two-week blow-out. I tried to be good, by joining a gym and making sure I only ate chicken after leaving the nightclubs and bars each evening. The fact that it was a whole, rotisserie-cooked chicken, at a time when some people would have been eating breakfast, makes it difficult for me to justify that I was being sensible, but I did my best! Most of us regularly weight trained during the holiday, before meeting up for an organised booze cruise or independent pub-crawl. It was during one such evening that a sales rep convinced us to head for a particular nightclub, after spotting our ripped bodies. He explained that there was a first prize of a £1,000 to be had for the winner of a body-building competition, a prize that was up for grabs according to 'Pedro,' and the offer of free tickets ensured our early arrival to the nightclub!

The peer pressure for me to enter the competition from within our group, still didn't affect my decision. Instead, I compromised by agreeing to check the place out first, arriving around 9pm. We'd previously built up courage by downing several large Bacardi and Cokes, and a friend was the first to volunteer to enter the competition. I was beginning to feel a little braver, eventually convincing myself to sign up, after checking out several 'Rambo-type' rivals that were now prancing around the dance floor in a drunken state. Nature called and as I approached a darkened corner, giving access to a staircase to the toilets, I made out half a dozen men dressed in suits. This bunch of monsters were clearly professional body builders, one of whom I'm now convinced was 'Shadow' off the hit TV series Gladiators, hosted by Ulrika Jonsson some years later in the 1990s! It was then that I rushed back to my mates like a giddy teenager, encouraging the lads to drink up and evacuate the place as quickly as possible, but not before the lads took a quick trip to the loo, so that they could see the celebrities for themselves.

Unfortunately, bad management did raise its head yet again in 1984 when the annual and compulsory 'bonding trip,' to Hall and Woodhouse Brewery at Blandford Forum, took place. This was an evening social, where it was accepted that the staff would get us around the brewery tour in record time, so that we could meet up with the distillery management team to have a 'P... Up'. Getting tipsy enough to enjoy the selection of stale crisps and bowls of sour pickled onions was all part of the fun, and singing a few rugby and Field Gun songs was expected as part of the deal. Singing and midweek drinking was never an inspiring option for me, even as a seasoned rugby player, and the thought of visiting the brewery for a third time filled me with dread. Fortunately, the first trainer offered three of us an early lift back to Lee-On-Solent, knowing that the evening was probably going to be a little tedious, and I took up his offer, grateful for an early night.

The following morning as we mustered for a pep talk, the second trainer inexplicably decided to humiliate the three of us that had left early the previous evening. We were made to stand in front of the rest of the crew whilst being belittled as he lectured us on what it means to be part of a team, sticking together through thick and thin and about working hard and playing hard. I felt myself getting more and more aggrieved by his illogical mantra, particularly as I knew him very well and was aware of his ploys for firing people up. He was still probably hung over from the previous evening, making his Churchillian speech even more of a joke, his face now turning beetroot colour.

From the age of sixteen I'd managed to grow in stature by coping and accepting a macho philosophy of everything being character-building. I was now at an age where I was happy with my character, and the injustice of what he was about to do could have cost me my place in the team for that year, or worse. As he dismissed the rest of the crew the three of us prepared to receive our punishment, when he placed a sandbag, around each of our necks. We remained fully dressed in track training kit, consisting of a long-sleeved top, woollen trouser, gaiters and steel toe-capped boots. I said very little but my facial expressions must have spoken a thousand words, as I became infuriated at what was happening to us.

He was well aware that the first trainer had given us authority to return early from the brewery, but he still decided to punish us for a lack of loyalty to the team. I privately vowed that I would smack him with the sandbag if he mentioned the words 'character-building' but fortunately for both of us he didn't, and we completed the five-mile road and beach run with him cycling alongside us for some of the way. The first trainer apologised to us sometime later, convincing us that he was unaware of what had happened before it was too late. In my book, apologising is a good sign of character and I still respect him for that, but we never received an apology from the second trainer.

It was a privilege to have competed during these times, and a special invite followed, when we were asked to give a display at two-military tattoos in Denmark, in August 1984. The visit was quite relaxing as we were racing against our 'B Crew', as a form of exhibiting the sport, albeit on the soft ground of a football pitch which proved difficult at times. But the highlight of the trip for me was seeing Arnold Schwarzenegger, close up, as he socialised with his body-building training staff at a city centre nightclub in Copenhagen one evening.

The trip got off to a poor start when most of us ran out of our allocated daily food vouchers after breakfast. We were billeted at an army camp and, unusually were given vouchers for our meals that should have lasted for the duration of the trip. The Danish Army had obviously never met Field Gunners before and within two days of our ten-day trip, our trainer requested an emergency meeting with officials to plead for additional food, which was duly granted and the scheme was scrapped. Happy days!

Serious injuries are a regular part of any crew's experience, but to hear of a death in the sport was a real shock. The incident involved a young man who held the same position as me, 'The Flying Angel', in the Portsmouth 'B crew' of 1982. Apparently, during the last part of the 'run back' the sailor continued to run through the middle of two sheer legs that formed an 'A frame', rather than stopping to allow the rig to collapse. It was the combined weight of the two legs at three-hundred-and-forty pounds, plus the additional force of the timbers being pulled downwards, when the fatality occurred, as the solid pieces of wood hit the unfortunate young man.

The unofficial motto in the Royal Navy was 'work hard play hard'; this was even more so when we were part of the Field Gun crew. I didn't have any interests, other than fitness training or sport, so as a seventeen-year-old boy I was considered unusual and naïve for not socialising during midweek or trying to get off with women. I looked forward to weekend parties, had close friends, but generally remained insular, not quite fitting in with my muscular image of the macho Field Gunner. My highlight of the weekend tended to be all about calories and how many I could devour at any one sitting. I did have some interest from women, mainly from those that were already in long-term relationships, perhaps wanting to be the first to test my innocence, whilst others were just content to flirt with me, creating problems on occasions. However, I was still content to wait until I met the woman of my dreams, and someone that I could consider marrying, but for reasons that I'm no longer proud of, my view of a relationship changed over the coming year, as I will explain in due course.

My first involvement in 1978 was very tough, and after participating in two further tournaments and from what I heard about subsequent crews, the following years seemed far easier. Most crew members from 1978 chose to never return again, and if they did it was because we were asked to, with a promise that things would definitely be better. This season was as long as any on record, beginning the first week of January right through to the end of August. The pressure of eliminations started within a few weeks of arriving at camp and ran right through to late April, before the group was whittled down to the last forty crew-members. However, the extra effort required to get through the fitness training compared to other years, was due in part to its tedious, repetitive nature that dulled the mind and senses. The monotony continued as we topped up our levels of fitness with sprints and light weight training, with minimal variation to our schedule, throughout the rest of our time on the track and during competition at Earl's Court.

Any encouragement that we received was based solely on making us tougher, fitter or faster, and the second trainer inspired me to perform to my physical limits, as he was confident that I could become a Royal Navy athletics sprinter. But, within three weeks I'd hit a brick wall as my speed decreased, at the same time as my muscle mass developed, due to the increased reps and amount of weights I was lifting. I felt totally drained and burnt out, as my body struggled to adapt to the drastic weight gain of a stone-and-a-half, but my mind remained focussed. The fact that I was an immature seventeen-year-old boy in a big man's body did little to improve my confidence, although I rarely allowed my guard to slip, and I felt that expectations of me were raised even more, based purely on my muscular appearance. There was very little, if any, emotional or psychological understanding of what was going on from staff or me, but for the most part I thrived on my achievements, able and willing to deal with whatever task was thrown my way. However, future trainers mellowed after realising that expecting us to complete eight clean full runs every day, right up to a week before the competition, was counterproductive and soul-destroying. I'd like to believe that lessons were learnt from our mistakes, resulting in the physical training becoming far more varied but still as challenging. The following seasons were shortened, mainly due to manpower shortages, with quality rather than quantity being the order of the day, and some crews running as few as two to four runs several weeks prior to competing in London.

At the end of each season, volunteers from the Fleet Air Arm crew were sought to act as guides, or commonly known as 'dogs', for members of a charity called St Dunstan's. In 1978 the attendees were all male, and blinded due to mistreatment and malnutrition, after being forced to construct the Burmese railway by the Japanese, during the Second World War. The whole of HMS Daedalus was shut down for the summer leave period, manned by a skeleton crew, and the week-long break helped the veterans rest and recuperate as they indulged in an active social programme.

Most events were held in the various senior rates bars, supplemented with organised day trips. It was accepted as a rewarding, life-changing experience to be a carer for them, something I only really appreciated three years later after volunteering again. By 1981, the demographic had changed, and we were now seeing far younger personnel at the camp, injured following IRA terrorist attacks. The men were all very smartly dressed, with a real desire to make the most of the freedom on offer, their primary focus based on how much they could drink each day. At my first camp, now aged eighteen, I was actively encouraged to take advantage of the free drinks that were on offer, and my immaturity got the better of me when I drank excessively each day. On two separate occasions I drank so much Port, then Rum and Black, that I became violently ill, blacked out, and required help getting back to my Mess. The long-term effect of my overindulgence, has put me off drinking both spirits ever since.

We only ever heard snippets of information about what had happened to the St Dunstan veterans during the war, but then it was often their friends telling the stories about another individual's trials and tribulations. As Field Gunners, it's perhaps something we should learn from, when we are tempted to get carried away to exaggerate about how hard things were for us. It was many years later before I realised what a lovely, honourable thing it was to do, being responsible for the care of an elderly blind and vulnerable war veteran. I therefore feel privileged again to be able to help my wife's ninety-two-year-old stepmum, Beryl, and her ninety-seven-year-old father, Fred, who themselves are partially blind. What an incredible generation these people are a part of, and what a fitting tribute to Fred, having recently been awarded a 'Legion d'Honneur' medal for his role in collecting vital information whilst posted in Europe during the second world war, and something none of the family were fully aware of until recently.

Let's not forget that Field Gun was an inaccessible sport to those outside of the Royal Navy. Even the Royal Marines and Commissioned Officers were exempt, and we may never have got selected to take part ourselves if alternative groups had been allowed access. In fact, since the Brickwoods competition has been opened up to some Army establishments, their recent success in winning first prize seems to support my theory. I understand that to many of us the accomplishment of representing our command, whether as an A or B crew member is the pinnacle of our physical endeavours, an achievement to cherish, and something to be immensely proud of.

We should feel very fortunate and privileged that we were in the right place at the right time and that we were probably fitter than most people will ever be. I'm grateful to have had the opportunity to be involved in such an incredible activity, with a great bunch of men that can be easily forgiven for allowing their ego and pride to get the better of them, on the odd occasion. I'm not sure many sports would function as effectively or efficiently as Field Gun did, given the amount of niggling injuries that we were expected to carry day in, day out over such a long season.

Playing any sport can be tough at times, and if a more scientific assessment could be achieved based on speed, endurance, strength, agility, skill level and physicality, I am confident that Field Gun would be considered far harder than most! Whatever the result, I am confident that we were and still are highly thought of and respected for carrying out one of the toughest sports in the world – or should that be one of the toughest **team** sports in the world?

During the early part of 1987, I was asked if I'd return for a fourth time, having been assured that the trainer could arrange a short extension of time on my Royal Navy leaving date, from May up to August. I was now focussed and looking forward to leaving the forces after handing in my notice some eighteen months earlier, so I kindly declined the offer. Instead, I began a four-week residential course in sales and marketing at Catterick Army camp in preparation to leave the Navy.

For reasons only the Government of the time could justify, funding for the Royal Tournament was withdrawn in 1999. This worldwide marketing extravaganza for the British Armed Forces was brought to an abrupt halt, making the sport of Field Gun redundant and confining it to the history books. Thanks to the hard work of a few committed ex Field Gunners, there is still a thriving association, and enough support to justify an annual reunion held in Coventry.

Returning the traveller at full speed

Preparing to drop on the ramp, ready for balancing on the raveller for some of the crew to pull me over the chasm

Carrying out the Flying Angel

Rig collapsing on the run back

Whipping the cable out of the chasm after carrying out the Flying Angel

Winners at last after representing the Fleet Air Arm Field Gun Crew for the third time. Glyn, 4th from right, middle row

Trekking in Nepal;
Mt Everest in the distance

Glyn and son, Rory;
base camp Mt Everest
2017

Fred with his Légion d'Honneur
medal

Chapter Six

MIGHTY OAKS FROM LITTLE ACORNS GROW

'**M**ighty Oaks from Little Acorns grow' was the motto for Myers Grove Comprehensive School, Stannington, Sheffield. The words were written in Latin, around a woven pair of acorns, and formed the school badge on our blazer pockets. I guess that the words were carefully selected to encourage, inspire, and motivate both pupils and staff to achieve high standards of education in the hope that some would become pillars of the community.

I recently researched the motto, anticipating that there would be several famous people mentioned in the school's role of honour! Instead, I came across the heading 'Notable Former Pupils' with only one name under it, Kate Botley. I've heard her on radio and watched her on TV. She's personable and witty but it doesn't say a lot for my old school when we only have one person to shout about. I'm sure that there are more famous people who have come through the school ranks, but you don't have to achieve fame to be valued, and each and every person is valued by God even as a little acorn or a Mighty Oak.

As a lean, but keen eleven-year-old boy, little did I know that within less than five years I'd grow into a six-foot-tall youth, with few qualifications and very little ambition to do anything with my life. Nevertheless, with the blessing of hindsight and after my Christian conversion many years later, I've learnt to be grateful for just being who God made me to be, and discovered that life is much more than being about how 'big or famous' you are, how 'bright' you come across to people, or how much money you're worth. Achievements, count for nothing if the One who gave you the gift isn't glorified.

Jeremiah ch.29, v.11-13 says,

"For I know the plans I have for you" declares the Lord, "plans to prosper you and not to harm you, plans to give you hope and a future. Then you will call on me and come and pray to me, and I will listen to you. You will seek me and find me when you seek me with all your heart."

The following pages will lead you down a path that was never 'my plan, vision or strategic goal', as I was never brought up to have 'big plans or dreams'. Things just seemed to happen, fall into place at the right time – or not – and doors opened or slammed shut to get me to where I was eventually able to say 'Thank you Lord, for each and every blessing that you've ever given me.'

I never considered my father to be a role model, in the truest sense of the word, as I rarely received encouragement, guidance, attention or affection from him. If anything, I just loved him for who he was, accepting that he would always be there for me if needed. I think Dad thought that I might follow him into the steel industry, as he took me to his workplace on one occasion when I was a very young boy. My recollection of that visit was that I played with feral cats all day, whilst Dad attended to staff requests for products from over the store counter.

My father's work ethic allowed me to eventually admire him rather than take him for granted, based on his devotion to ensure that the family always had a meal on the table, even when he went through some difficult times, whilst earning very little in the process. The only thing that I knew about my dad's childhood was that he was called up for National Service for the RAF and based at an airfield near Blackpool, that he was part of the school football team, and that Mum was his first and only girlfriend. I taunted him about how many airplanes he must have cleaned each day whilst in the RAF, as he seemed to have forgotten exactly what he did when serving. I never felt pressurised to live up to any expectations or driven to achieve results; instead, it was always considered adequate that I did the best I could and accepted what I had. Dad worked long hours for a poor wage whilst Mum looked after the home and brought up me and my sister, who was four-and-a-half years younger. As far as my father's working environment was concerned, I don't think that he ever wanted promotion, could cope with much responsibility, or would have welcomed change. He was also exploited by his employers, in my opinion, as were many working-class people of the time.

There were no school clubs or extracurricular activities, prior to attending comprehensive school, and my eagerness to compete soon became evident when I left junior school. Although I had a love for football, I was soon playing for the school under-12 rugby team, making my debut at inside-centre. As my skills developed, I played for South Yorkshire under-16s, before going on to a Yorkshire trial at the same age group, against Hull and East Riding. I also held the school record each year up to under-14 level, for shot and discus, although I found athletics very tedious, disliking it intensely. My enthusiasm for team sports also allowed me to make up the numbers for the school cricket and basketball teams, but my physical development stalled for a while when I became a teenager.

My Yorkshire under-16 trial ended when I suffered severe concussion, after my opposite number hit me square on the jaw. Some minutes earlier, one of our players had been upended after a dangerous tackle and his foot landed directly on to the top of my head, making me partially concussed, but without anyone noticing. Our team had earlier identified that my opposite number shouldn't be messed with, standing well over six feet tall, muscular, with a shaven head and more side burn than I've ever been able to grow in a lifetime. Play was stopped to assess any injuries to the victim of the bad tackle, when I began walking over to the opposition centre, in a dream-like state. Approaching him unnoticed, I gave him a shove in the chest, resulting in him smacking me straight on the chin and putting my lights out for over fifteen minutes. I received no medical treatment, but I did receive a 'rollicking' from Mr Snell when I came around, for starting a fight! I found out recently, whilst chatting to an old school friend at a wedding, that it was a common occurrence for schools to put older players forward for selection at representative level. As boys' ages weren't sufficiently checked by the committees of the day, I'm convinced that my opposite number was older than fifteen!

I finished school in the summer of 1976, keen to enjoy life but still not knowing whether or not I'd been accepted to join the Royal Navy. I had no set plans, happy to follow, rather than lead, with no GCSE qualifications to my name. I'd lost my enthusiasm for education two years earlier, when the way we were taught changed drastically in the space of a term. From teachers seemingly enjoying explaining subjects in a practical and dynamic way, dictation and large amounts of homework became the standard method of teaching. The result of this experience was catastrophic, as far as my exam results were concerned. It meant that in five short months I had dropped from ranking second to thirtieth, in a class of thirty- two pupils. School, therefore, became a tedious necessity from an educational viewpoint, but still my place of belonging as far as friendships and playing sport were concerned.

Missing school never crossed my mind, and I was only ever absent due to illness when I had tonsillitis on three occasions, and supported by the fact that I refused to 'wag' school in 1972 when a group of fifth-form lads tried bullying younger pupils. It was their intention to get as many boys as possible to boycott school in order to watch an early mid-week football match. This would have enabled us to watch Pele play for Santos against Sheffield Wednesday, down the road at Hillsborough. Due to power cuts at that time the football club were unable to use their floodlights for an evening kick off.

Between leaving upper school to joining the Royal Navy, our milkman, Ryan, offered me a cash-in-hand job as his assistant. I worked from 5.30am until 10.30am, five days a week for £1.50 a shift. At the same time, I collected an additional £7.70 weekly unemployment allowance and paid my parents £5 for board and lodgings. Ryan ran a farm with his wife, but he fancied himself as a Formula 1 driver and playboy. He collected me on a few evenings to go out drinking, with the blessing of my parents who trusted him to take care of me. However, he would rendezvous with a young lady friend, who would plonk herself on my lap in the front of his pickup van, before we ventured to a deserted country pub. The pair would flirt with each other throughout the evening, using me as their decoy in case his wife ever started asking questions.

Another time, we went out for a quiet drink without picking up his friend, but on our return journey, and as darkness fell, he switched off the van lights and then sped through the remote countryside roads at break neck speed. He insisted that it would be easy to see other vehicles coming towards us, as their headlight beams would be spotted well in advance. With no seat belt, I hung on to the seat with all of my strength, as fear struck me cold.

It was that same evening when we visited the Sheffield red-light area where he drove around the streets of Broomhall, pointing out the ladies of the night, as if he knew them personally. I was fascinated by the experience, particularly as he seemed so relaxed and familiar with the area, allowing himself a cheeky smirk when I asked if he'd ever been with any of them. We drove off, but only when he sensed that I was getting concerned about the predicament I found myself in and how late it was getting. Within six years the headlines in the national press stated that Peter Sutcliffe, the Yorkshire Ripper, had been arrested in the same area that we'd visited.

The few weeks spent working with Ryan helped to build up my fitness levels. I would carry as many milk bottles as possible in the hand-held carrying crates, whilst running back and forth between houses and his van. It was always expected that as soon as I began to earn money I should pay 'my way' for lodgings. This helped in creating a strong sense of respect for hard-earned cash, and to a lesser degree some years previously, when my parents encouraged me to always save a part of my spending money. These habits have served me well throughout my lifetime, enabling me to seriously consider retiring from full-time work when I approached fifty-five years of age.

In a roundabout way, Dad was instrumental in guiding me towards joining the Fleet Air Arm, when he asked his friend to meet with me, after coming home on leave from the Royal Navy. I sensed that he was getting concerned about my future, which was justified, due in part to my reaction after finishing my last careers lesson at school. The lesson itself was always one where scribbling on a desk was more stimulating than anything the teacher had to say, until he asked what we were all going to do when we left school, in ten months' time.

I genuinely didn't have a clue where my future lay, but I was shocked when all of my closest friends knew exactly what they wanted to do, some already having apprenticeships in place. Arriving back home, I felt deflated and surprised that most of my mates had got plans without letting me know. It seemed an age away before we finished our school education, and I enjoyed living day by day without a care in the world. I was reasonably bright, reflected in me being in the top stream of classes all through my time at school. But I'd now given up on education, finishing my History GCSE in a record ten minutes, which two years previously had been one of my best subjects.

I'd been convinced to join a foreign police force by my friend Barry, who was an exile at the time, ready to fly out to Rhodesia (now called Zimbabwe) to become an armed motorbike cop. The ambition or fantasy to travel so far away soon subsided, but the local police force was still a brilliant option, as far as I was concerned. The turning point came when Dad told me that, "you can never trust a copper, plus you'll never have any friends if you become one." Why my Dad thought this is a mystery, and I've had several friends who've served in the police force, to be able to disagree with his assumption.

He'd previously only ever had positive encounters with the police. Firstly, when they had escorted the ambulance rushing me to the children's hospital in an emergency, and then, much later in a fraud investigation at work, which he'd initiated against two rogue managers. As someone who was always looking for approval before I'd commit to something, hearing those damning words against the police force influenced me to dismiss a career path in that direction. I'd already given up hope of ever becoming a Physical Education teacher when a sports teacher told me that I would have to study for another subject, like Maths or English, to qualify. Therefore, any hope of a career guided by my interests or passions had evaporated.

Nevertheless, I was still only fifteen when I was selected from our year group, along with another boy, to attend a four-day residential placement. This was presented to me as being a school acquaint course for the Royal Navy, held at HMS Dryad in Hampshire, as a prize given out by our headmaster for good behaviour. I can't recall how I got there or back or much else about what we did, except that on my return I vowed that I'd never join the Royal Navy in a million years. However, nine months later Dad arranged a meeting with his closest friend, Ray, who had served most of his twenty-two years in the Royal Navy at sea. He understood that I was a keen sportsman, so encouraged me to apply to join the Fleet Air Arm rather than opting for a General Service role, explaining that personnel within the Fleet Air Arm rarely went to sea, and that I would be able to play as much sport as I wanted to.

On a hot summer's day in August 1976, I joined up as an Aircraft and Engines Mechanic in the Royal Navy's Fleet Air Arm. Earning £22 per fortnight, after tax, food and accommodation expenses, and having access to numerous sporting activities, it seemed like I was in heaven on earth. Nevertheless, after learning to hate exams at school, over the next eleven years I avoided as many courses or exams as I could. Instead I undertook to kick, pull, throw, paddle, lift or hit anything whenever possible, as an expression of my love of sport.

During a junior recruits' expedition to Bethesda in Wales, I was first observed to see if I had what it took to become a Physical Training instructor, as most people who knew me thought this was an obvious fit. In truth, when I was asked to lead a short workout before breakfast, I was as nervous as could be, lacking the confidence to project any authority over the rest of the group. Still, the instructors were encouraging with their comments and told me to continue to pursue my ambition. Such was my energy and greed for anything physical, that on one of the treks around the Welsh mountains I asked our instructor how far we had to walk. He responded by saying that 'it wasn't too far, Wood', and that it would be easy for someone as fit as me, even with a full rucksack. I retorted, saying that 'it wasn't the distance, Sir, but rather the boredom of having to walk.' I was allowed to continue, after seeking permission to run ahead to advanced points so that I could wait for the group to catch me up. A week of activities, including some new experiences, like abseiling and rock-climbing, ended with our final night sleeping in a bat infested cave. By the time I returned back to camp, I realised that I disliked responsibility and was happier to be playing sport rather than teaching it.

Within a couple of years of joining up, it seemed that I'd been taken out of circulation from normal naval life, without anyone realising it, as I was spending months away playing sport or partaking in Field Gun training. It felt as though I was being promoted as a professional sportsman at times, something that suited me, but the impact was becoming quite damaging behind the scenes! So much so that my trade training suffered and I got lost in the system for months on end, avoiding camp duties and trade exams that were compulsory! Things came to a head when I returned to Yeovilton and was ordered to report to the Lynx training squadron chief, who instantly put me forward for my qualified-to-maintain and qualified-to-sign exams, but without having had any experience of working on the helicopters! This was always going to end in failure and after a retake of one exam, I was threatened with dismissal from the Navy if I failed again. It was only then that a supervisor came alongside me and looked at why I was failing, eventually spending time to explain fully how the systems worked, which was enough for me to pass comfortably some days later.

Around the same time, my rugby career was in full flow, but a poor performance got the better of my emotions when I played in an England regional trial game, for Combined Services Colts against the South West. I was now an established winger, aged eighteen with my seniors predicting a big future for me, having recently been moved from outside centre to fast-track my opportunities to play for the full Navy team. The match was played during the winter on a misty, ice-cold day, where most of the play was taking place in the forwards, all happily steaming and puffing around, whilst I froze on the far touchline. For the first time in the game I received the ball, only to drop it due to my fingers being numb with cold. To me, my rugby career was over, my enthusiasm for the sport totally dissolving as the minutes ticked by without touching the ball again. Returning back to base disillusioned, I notified the HMS Heron, rugby team captain that I was going to stop playing the sport altogether. I'd had a further disappointment the previous Easter, when a message to go on tour with the full Royal Navy team got to me too late and I'd not been contacted since, so as far as I was concerned my mind was made up.

My lack of enthusiasm didn't last long, as I was informally ordered to turn up for the next camp game on the following Wednesday afternoon. Being greeted with the No.8 shirt left me concerned, particularly when I was told to scrum down and stick my head between the back sides of the two biggest, ugliest players on the park and to follow the No.7 around the pitch wherever he went. Our No.7, or open-side wing-forward, was a current Royal Navy flanker who'd played at a good level for many years, a much-admired man, modest in all that he did. I couldn't have asked for a better mentor, although I was shocked one time when we played against each other, to receive a thump to my face at a lineout, for no other reason than to see if I could take a bit of niggle, now that I was a forward!

I thrived as a back-row player, enjoying the involvement, fortunate enough to have the skill sets to make a difference and exert some influence in most games. However, to change position was a big gamble, particularly as expectations of me as a winger, had been growing immeasurably. I thrived in my new position, so much so, that I began travelling to Kettering at the weekends after been invited to do so by a friend, to play social rugby for the fourth team. I was quickly selected to play for the first team and made a good impression, scoring a try on my debut against Kenilworth and awarded with man of the match. That same season we went on to win The East Midlands Cup Final against Stockwood Park.

Things got even better when I was selected to play for Combined Services versus British Police at blind-side wing-forward in 1981, before I'd played for the Royal Navy senior side, and I quickly made the No.6 or No.8 positions my own thereafter. Time away and several injuries limited me to just eight appearances at Twickenham, in the Inter-Service Championship, and it was a relief to win my first cap against the Army in 1983. My pride at being selected to play for Combined Services against Canada in the same year and coming off the bench to play against Australia in 1984, still didn't match the feelings I had when I won my naval cap, but I relished them all.

My lack of willingness to study and contentment at being almost a full-time sportsman, meant that my prospects for career advancement in the Royal Navy got sidelined, but I wouldn't have swapped my life for anything. Promotion through the ranks during my naval career meant little, but earning money meant a lot. I therefore found ways to subsidise my earnings at every opportunity, although some of the things I did were frowned upon and probably flaunted military regulations at times. Industrious business ventures included renovating a motorbike to sell on, selling training shoes, managing the tuck shop on my department, and working on the doors of pubs and nightclubs, sometimes three times a week. By the age of twenty-two I had a 50% ownership of a house in Weymouth with a friend, and I was renting out rooms to fellow sailors. All of this extra income allowed me to buy my own place three years later. In a further attempt to boost my income, I passed a ships diver's aptitude test in 1983, something that would have allowed me to apply to become a fully trained ship's diver and receive a small financial retainer for the rest of my naval career. However, during the test I found myself in some quite fearful situations that I didn't enjoy, almost running out of air at one time, after failing to equalise the oxygen bottles correctly. I thought it best not to pursue any further involvement with diving thereafter, and I decided that it was far easier and safer to carry out a rent review or charge a little extra for a pair of trainers!

Establishing myself as a confident Aircraft and Engines Mechanic was difficult, but I was competent enough to muddle through and be awarded the Flag Officer Third Flotilla Proficiency Award, for outstanding achievement, just before I left the service. It's a prestigious award that very few naval personnel ever achieve, and one that my squadron commander put me forward for when I transformed the ground equipment department on 815 squadron. The section had previously been a dumping ground of leaking and badly maintained equipment, which I turned into a pristine, well-equipped holding area, where everything became accounted for. Up until this time, I'd rarely valued my competitiveness and the character-building qualities that playing sport was developing in me, due in part, to the fact that I'd never been paid for playing sport. I'd always looked at something with value as having a price tag attached to it, and although the transformation of the ground equipment department took vision, guile, negotiation and favours, most of all it required lots of energy and perseverance. It seemed that at the eleventh hour, I'd found something other than rugby to stimulate me, and probably creating a realisation that I'd been undervaluing my entrepreneurial tendencies!

Upon leaving the Royal Navy, my salary was £8,000 per year, and I spoke to Dad about whether he thought I'd ever earn that amount of money again, in Civvy Street. I didn't think that it was a big wage but his response caught me by surprise, when he said that he'd never earned anywhere near that amount. This allowed me to realise just how tough times had really been for my parents, supporting our family on a meagre wage, yet at the same time they were content with their lot, something I wasn't...yet content with.

Within a year of leaving the forces I'd almost doubled my earnings as the top salesman for Black Horse Estate Agency in Bedford, which was part of the Lloyds Bank Group. I found the work exhilarating, competitive, and loved the idea that the harder you worked the more commission you were paid, taking great delight in writing to a Chief Petty Officer who said that I'd never survive in Civvy Street, to let him know that I was now earning as much as him. The person in question was apparently embarrassed by the letter, but still let everyone he supervised see it. Unsurprisingly, they ribbed him for days afterwards. He had hated the fact that I played rugby for the Royal Navy or Combined Services, and he would regularly remind me that it was futile to even ask for time off, whilst working under him. I didn't feel he personally disliked me, but he did enjoy the power to exert his authority on those that were of a lesser rank, just for the sake of it.

On one such occasion I was servicing our Lynx helicopter, when he approached me to say that he'd been handed a signal, requesting that I be released from duty to play for the Royal Navy rugby team in two days' time. We'd only just arrived back at base that week, after flying from the ship after a deployment away, so it was refreshing to know that the selectors were keeping an eye on me, even though I was struggling to retain my match fitness. He abruptly told me that I wouldn't be released under any circumstances, but he was fighting a losing battle, as my squadron commander was himself a keen rugby supporter and enjoyed the prestige of having a Royal Navy and Combined Services player under him. Needless to say, the Chief Petty Officer was summoned to a meeting and returned moments later, scowling, as he reluctantly told me to go and sort out my travel arrangements for the match. Feeling well-supported by the other members on my flight, allowed me to never feel too guilty about the time I had off, but I appreciate that it was probably a hindrance regularly losing a member of such a small group of tradesmen.

I'd always had an interest in property from a very young age, and the prospect of buying and selling anything, in the hope of making a profit, excited me. Through good fortune, I was able to gain a foothold on the property ladder from the age of twenty-two, when a friend told me that he was ready to sell his half-share in a large Victorian terraced house, in Gloucester Street, Weymouth. So, with very little fuss

I obtained a mortgage, and by the time I left Weymouth aged twenty-seven, Alison and I were able to buy a brand-new detached home in Kettering, when we married in 1987. Fortunately, Alison had also bought a rundown house a few years earlier, enabling her to make a substantial profit when she sold it after only three years. I was excited about the future, as I hoped to at last fulfil my ambition of becoming a policeman, particularly when I was offered a direct link to a senior officer in the Metropolitan Police. The Navy rugby team had played against the Met at Imber Court, some weeks prior to me leaving the forces, when the committee members from both teams must have been discussing my future prospects. Working in London appealed to me, as it wasn't too far away from Northamptonshire to be able to commute, or Alison and I could eventually move there if the need arose. The Chief Constable had given me his direct dial telephone number, urging me to ring him if I was genuinely serious about joining the force. I'd already been discussing with some friends how best to apply for the Northamptonshire police force, but I'd been discouraged after realising that they didn't take applicants who wore glasses.

Fortunately, the Met Police's restrictions were far less stringent, and my hopes were bolstered after receiving such encouraging signs from my contact. I was asked to get a prescription from an optician, then to report the results through to the Chief Constable, which I did. His response ended any dreams that I had of ever becoming a policeman, when he said "You're f***ing blind, how do you play rugby?" After building up my hopes, thinking that I'd be an ideal candidate for policing the country's streets, I was left despondent. Further bad news followed as my enquiries to join the fire and prison services all came back saying that there were no immediate vacancies. However, whilst short-lived, I was given a real boost to my confidence when I was interviewed to be a paramedic. Paramedics were a relatively new thing for the Northants ambulance service, and the interviewer was elated to have such a young, fit serviceman applying for the position. After the interview, I sensed that the job was mine for the taking, the officer encouragingly advising me that I'd get a response within the next week. A letter arrived some days later, at my home in Weymouth, with a simple message stating that my application had been rejected. Perplexed to receive such a response, I still felt unable to ring the station through embarrassment. Instead, I visited the local ambulance station in Weymouth, and spoke to an officer informally.

I explained that I was trying to make sense of the whole situation after being so encouraged, and his immediate response was to ask if I'd got a criminal record, which I hadn't. It turned out that the penalty points on my driving licence had been detected some time after the interview, at a time when jobs were in short supply and most employers could afford to be as choosy as they wished.

By January of 1987 and in desperation, I researched how to become a bodyguard and considered working full-time on the doors of night clubs, something I'd done previously part-time, but deep down I knew these jobs weren't really for me. Because of time served in the Royal Navy, I was allowed to partake in up to four weeks of free educational or career training before leaving the forces. I'd always got a thrill from selling things, then detected that a vast majority of the Telegraph and Times newspaper job supplements were advertising sales or marketing positions. I therefore chose to do a sales and marketing course, based at Catterick army camp. I'd only recently left Northampton Saints to join Bedford rugby club, and I was already earning additional income by selling a range of sportswear. But I was taken aback by the efforts of the committee at Bedford rugby club to ensure that I felt looked after, as I was sent several leads for jobs and given an informal interview by the manager of the Bedford branch of Black Horse Estate Agents, called Stimpsons. The interview was productive and I was advised that the position of Sales Negotiator would be coming up in the near future, that it would include on-the-job training, but would be more about my determination to succeed rather than anything else. A second interview was set up with the Area Manager, who concluded that I was an ideal candidate and had given one of the best interviews he'd ever been part of.

Prior to being accepted as an Estate Agent, I was told by my career's advisor from the Navy that gaining experience in interview techniques was crucial. I therefore applied for several jobs that I had no intention of pursuing, allowing me to understand what companies were looking for in a candidate, and as a way to learn how to control my nerves. This experience proved invaluable, so much so that on one occasion, having been interviewed by two Directors in their boardroom, I had them in stitches. It felt like an interrogation as one would ask questions whilst the other's piercing eyes gave me the once-over from the other side of the table. I felt uneasy, as it proved difficult to engage with both men at the same time. It turned out that their company had been involved in a construction project installing underground fuel tanks at my last posting in Portland, so I knew the terrain of the air base well. I made this known to them, before casually mentioning that some months earlier the Ministry of Defence were investigating why the fuel tanks had been leaking. Their look of concern, followed by a change of demeanour, effectively supported with expletives, gave away how vulnerable they were feeling. I quickly confirmed that I was joking with them, the three of us now totally relaxed, as we all laughed together. From this point on the interview was far less formal as they were keen to know more about my rugby career, than anything else. It turned out that they were season-ticket holders at Bedford and their company a main sponsor. There wasn't a current job vacancy, but they seemed happy enough with me to say that they'd contact me again if one came up.

It was a relief to learn some weeks later, that I'd got a job offer to join Stimpsons. Due to an economic down turn I left the company in 1991 as an Assistant Manager, but I missed the thrill of viewing, valuing and selling the wonderful array of property that I was fortunate enough to visit. During my time at the office, I learnt that military humour wasn't always appreciated in some cases! This became particularly obvious when our senior valuer was asked to train me to carry out market appraisals on a variety of properties. It was still late morning when we attended the last of our pre-booked valuations, and he asked me to stay in the car whilst he popped into a house to get some final measurements. I turned around from the passenger's seat to see a transparent sandwich box resting on the rear car seats, full of goodies. Without hesitation I took a bite from an apple, meticulously placing it back in the sealed container, so the bite mark was hidden. We returned to the office and he went for his lunch break. Knowing what he was about to find in his lunch box, I began to giggle, which created suspicious gazes from the rest of the office staff. A few moments passed before he appeared down the stairs from the first floor, looking rather emotional as he stared over towards me. I couldn't contain my laughter any longer when he asked, "Why have you taken a bite of my apple?", but I remember feeling rather awkward by his reaction as tears flowed down my cheeks, not quite knowing how to answer him. I soon got over feeling too sympathetic, reminding him that he was fortunate to have anything left, never mind a bite missing from his apple, as any food left unattended in the forces is consumed by others within seconds.

The Government announced that joint-tax relief on mortgages was being halted, from August 1988. This meant that only one person living at a property would get tax relief on the first £30,000 of their mortgage, rather than any partners living together, getting relief on £30,000 each. The housing market crashed overnight and within eighteen months of starting my job as an estate agent, my position was now in jeopardy, at a time when I'd had a serious neck injury playing rugby, and other injuries were beginning to take their toll. It was time to re-evaluate our future, after announcing that I would be stepping down as captain of Bedford at the end of the 1991 season. We'd made a decision that I would set up my own business, carrying out garden and property clearances, whilst also being a househusband and looking after our ten-month old daughter, Natasha. I told my accountant that I would probably earn about £12,000 pa, plus we had the security of Alison's teaching job to tide us over. To further reduce our outgoings, we cashed in several insurance policies and re-mortgaged our house, on what was an incredible deal at the time, set at 10.2% over two years.

Within weeks of setting up the business it became evident that the best-laid plans were failing on all fronts. I wasn't a natural househusband, plus Alison's heart was breaking at the thought of not being able to bring up our daughter, particularly after being such an incredible mum during her maternity leave from teaching. In addition, my hunger to make the business succeed was being impaired by missed opportunities that I didn't have time to follow up. I began struggling to find the time to fit all of my jobs in, so we therefore made the bold decision for Alison to hand in her notice, allowing her to become the best mother anyone could ask for. This allowed me to funnel all of my energy into the business, turning over £80,000 in its first year rather than my predicted £12,000. I was still able to enjoy rugby by coaching the forwards at Kettering, and I was grateful for the way that the rugby club chairman encouraged me with my business at this time, introducing me to several positive leads.

Being a leader didn't come naturally and I've never had any management training, preferring to avoid leadership positions on occasions, but enjoying growing into roles at other times. My speedy promotion to Assistant Manager at Stimpsons upset some people, due to my lack of experience in the job, but it was based on my passion to sell and beat my targets that shone through.

Playing rugby, I always knew that my tactical skills were far less developed than my ability with the ball in hand, or open play in general, a by-product of never having been part of a settled team or having had regular one-to-one coaching since school. Recognising my lack of teaching inspired me to take my Rugby Football Union, Preliminary Coaching Award in 1986, and going back to the basics of rugby was refreshing. I'm astounded how the game has developed technically, as it seems that most senior players now know how, why and when they should take ownership for their every move on the field, rather than the captain and coach taking full responsibility. A regular complaint of mine was that most forward coaches were props, focusing purely on line-outs and scrums, with very little input involving tactics or developing an individual's skill sets. It was therefore a privilege to be appointed vice-captain, then captain, when coached by a New Zealander, called Ian, during my last two years at Bedford. Ian was previously a backs coach with Taranaki, but from time to time he was able to call upon the services of a New Zealand Maori to help him out, who was himself a prop forward. Both took time out with me to introduce new techniques, look at how I could influence a game physically and mentally, and challenged me to question what the team were doing in different parts of the pitch and at different times during a game. We were introduced to a sports psychologist, and there was encouragement to attack from anywhere, to play a fast-paced, rucking game, and it was something I loved but frustratingly serious injuries limited my game time. I learnt more about playing rugby in my last two years, than I'd been taught in the previous eighteen, but neck, shoulder and back injuries eventually forced my early retirement. Nevertheless, the lessons learnt became an asset that I was able to pass on with some success, when I began coaching the forwards at Kettering Rugby Club in 1991.

As a rugby coach I always tried to base my decisions on what was best for the team, rather than what was best for any one individual, evident when at the start of my time as forwards' coach I left out several of the best players when they didn't turn up for training. Although risky, this proved a fruitful strategy, and one that eventually paid huge dividends for the club. As team ethic developed, we became a tough side to beat, winning promotion to Midlands Division 1 then upsetting all the forecasts by defeating a Leeds side away in the Pilkington Cup, a team that was many leagues above us. A further privilege was that I received an invite to coach the East Midlands rugby team for their County Championship campaign in 1994. It was something that I was keen to do by myself, to see if I had what it takes to be influential with backs as well as the forwards, as previously at Kettering I'd had very little input with the backs. A further incentive was that I was assured that I would be head coach when the East Midlands played in the annual Mobbs Memorial match, against The Barbarians, a representative team that always included several international players in their ranks. Traditionally, the Northampton coaching staff would take over for this prime fixture, selecting a team made up from Bedford and Northampton, so I was excited at the prospect of taking on the coaching responsibility myself. However, when the time came to play the fixture, I was told that the current Saint's coach, Ian McGeechan, would be taking over. His credentials as an international player and world class coach are as good as anyone, but I was treated poorly in my opinion, and although I received an apology, I was given no explanation as to why I'd been sidelined.

As the forward's coach at Kettering, I chose to keep my distance from most players when socialising, as I didn't want them to think I had favourites, and it was agreed that I didn't have to attend the selection meeting. It was left to the other coach, Doug, to give my input to the committee and those players that had been left out. It was therefore a real shock when I was voted clubman of the year, an award voted for by all the playing members of the club.

During this period, I found a new confidence in my decision-making, whether it was in business or leisure, taking calculated risks and trusting my judgement. There was a realisation that even if you have people following you who are less able or qualified than others, they can be as effective if they have the same vision, desire and passion as yourself.

From 1991, and thereafter, adapting quickly to fast changing circumstances became a key strength in keeping my small business afloat. This was particularly evident when I began to expand rapidly and then further developed the business into a well established limited company, carrying out building and maintenance contracts for insurance loss adjusters. There was always pressure on me to take a bigger geographical area on, by some of our clients, and this was something that appealed to my ego initially, particularly as I strived to reach a turnover target of £1,000,000. When the risk outweighed the reward, and with the help and advice of Alison, we made a conscious decision to offer a quality service, rather than chasing after more turnover and increasing our quantity of work. Although Alison was a director, her position was mainly part-time to include debt management and some of the day-to-day administration. But her most important role, that I valued as much as anything, was to ensure that the family was well looked after, and I would do my best to prioritise being home on time each evening for a hot meal, around the table with my wife and children. Ultimately, the responsibility and isolation of being the key decision maker was becoming ever more burdensome, as further regulations were introduced into the construction industry, making it difficult to make the time to think strategically. Instead, our clients introduced tougher health and safety criteria, regular audits and in effect began to dictate what and how we should do things. Having to deal with employment law issues, whilst being made to gain several national accreditations and making time for our business 'partners' to audit us, all led to additional pressure, as well as adding substantial, non-chargeable costs to our overheads.

Outside of business, by 2000 I'd been a committed Christian for around three years, when I was asked to consider putting my name forward for election as Church Warden at Christ the King Church, Kettering. Although, I was inexperienced in the nitty-gritty of Anglican churchmanship, my passion, faith and love of Christ Jesus was my motivation in every area of my life. I was duly elected onto the Parochial Church Council, as Warden, and although I knew most of the people on the Council, I still felt slightly awkward when I attended my first evening meeting. Our vicar, Rev. Mike Talbot, fully supported me, and it was he who had encouraged me to apply for the role. As most of those on the Council were professional people, they were familiar and well acquainted with board or staff meetings, and therefore used to management jargon, something that was alien to me. During the next six years, I learnt and began to rely on other qualities, such as patience, perseverance, self-control, kindness, and a better understanding of what it means to love thy neighbour. Managing volunteers and mixing with all age groups, with varied levels of ability, agendas and backgrounds enabled me to understand how we are all different, and it was a time when there was a realisation that 'maturity' didn't necessarily come with age, that we are all prone to mistakes, misunderstandings, stubbornness and pride, all of which can cloud our judgement no matter what age we are. It was a time when my faith and trust in following Jesus as my 'Lord and Saviour' developed, as I constantly found myself out of my comfort zone, whether in business or church leadership. I thank Mike wholeheartedly, for his support in giving me the opportunity to be part of church leadership, after just three years of attending church, when I know that people would have challenged him about the decision.

In a nutshell, it was my aim to show goodness in everything I did from then on. As far as I was concerned, it was a given that I could and would trust people on the Parochial Church Council, but in business I had to re-learn to put trust in my staff and particularly in the judgement of my managers. When trust is broken it's hard to recover from, even when you are able to forgive the person. This is something I had to do on numerous occasions. Several of my longest-serving employees let themselves down over the years, and it remains for them to answer why, but all denied any wrongdoing whilst evidence proved otherwise. I always felt a slight vulnerability, as I relied heavily on the staff's skill sets in construction or IT, gifts that I didn't possess. I was an open and loyal boss, expecting a good level of output to a high standard in return, but I'm convinced that some of those who took advantage mistook my generosity for naivety or weakness when it was ripe for them to exploit. Perhaps, it's just human nature to take advantage of situations as familiarity develops, but knowing where to draw a line before it's too late, is very difficult? Only three employees were ever sacked, all for theft, while other staff decided that it was best to leave rather than face the consequences of their deceit. On other occasions I persevered and remained patient with the damaging attitude that some people adopted, hoping that things might change, until eventually deciding, after twenty-one years in business, to sell the company in 2012.

I'm convinced that all the major decisions that I made were always well thought through and relevant, at the time they were implemented.

I enjoyed most of my time running the business and I had some lovely, committed personnel, but I felt it wise to always keep a certain distance between myself and employees.

It was during the 2008 economic collapse, when the rates that our main client offered to pay to us were suddenly reduced by 20%, and then again, by a further 20%, just six months later. I had to cut costs to give us a fighting chance to survive the downturn, so I set about looking at the fairest way to introduce changes. But, I was taken aback when I included both of my contract managers in the consultation process and it wasn't too long before one of the managers, Jim, who happened to be my longest serving employee, began to undermine the other manager, Steve. Being a pragmatic person, I confronted Steve about what I'd heard and it was immediately evident that the accusations against him were inappropriate, divisive and Jim was trying to protect his own position. After carrying out further investigations, which involved checking vehicle tracking and mobile phone data over the last six years, I had no other option but to confront Jim with the damning evidence about how he'd abused his position of trust and neglected his managerial position.

During this time I spoke to a close friend, Paul, who gave me an uneasy summary of his experience about employing staff, after I was reaching the end of my tether running the company. Paul had been a director himself, in a large company, and gave me the following advice. He said that as an employer your staff see you as their provider, giving them a living, and a roof over their head, and once that is threatened whatever's gone before counts for nothing. This proved prophetic, as with every consultation more members of our staff proved difficult to win over, leaving me perplexed, frustrated and disappointed, as I was convinced that they'd show a certain degree of loyalty. In a last-ditch attempt I disclosed our end-of-year figures, which confirmed that they'd all earned more than the combined wages of Alison and me, for that year. It was later revealed that Jim had influenced several of the staff to back him in what he perceived was a power struggle, but in an attempt to protect his own position, had led others to hand in their notice, in anticipation that we were going under! As consultations progressed, Jim sought the services of a union and insisted that he met me and Alison with his union representative, to discuss his proposed change of contract and challenge all of our proposals. But, by the end of the meeting the union rep actually agreed with all that we'd suggested, and advised the manager to accept the new terms. Jim eventually handed in his notice, when a few days later we provided evidence and confronted him about his deception, which spanned over more than six-years. He still felt it necessary to take one last dig at me and got his wife involved, who questioned my Christian values and accused me of unprofessionalism, after upsetting their child. It was alleged that the child had intercepted formal letters and emails from the company, that confirmed acceptance of the employee's resignation, and which they wanted to keep from her.

Another longstanding employee, called Ron, tried to take advantage during this time, and I was left feeling really disappointed by his behaviour, as I'd previously held his position open for over four months after he'd been seriously ill. He threatened me with intervention from a barrister's office for what they saw was a lack of consultation, it turned out that his daughter worked as a secretary at a solicitor's office and had clearly been misinformed about what process her father had been through with us. I felt scorned when he thought that he had me round his little finger and said, "Nothing personal, Glyn, but business is business, I want paying off with a redundancy package." I explained that I still needed him and that the money I would be paying out for his package alone accounted for all the savings I was making, across the whole company. Savings I had to make in order to try and preserve everyone's jobs during this economic downturn. We ran a professional business where employment law, health and safety and staff welfare were as important as the trade work they carried out, and I'd been guided by the services of a national company on how best to deal with our unfortunate position.

Although it was never my intention to lay anyone off permanently, I was thankful when both employees resigned after they were confronted with the truth, and I couldn't stop myself from saying to Ron, "no hard feelings, but business is business" (forgive me Lord). Sadly, a couple more personnel moved on and it was an exhausting time recovering from such an unforeseen set of circumstances. At some time, most, if not all had commented that it was the best job they'd ever had, and each year they'd all contributed towards a substantial Christmas gift for Alison and I, as a thank-you present . I can't thank the remaining staff enough for the way they adapted to get us through the crisis, particularly my remaining Contract Manager, a real God-send and the man originally accused of shirking his duties by the other two employees.

Throughout this time of struggle and conflict, I always felt close to God, and as my emotions swung back and forth between feeling despondent then elated, my faith remained strong. However, it was only with hindsight that I was able to look back and see how God had been there with me, and as importantly, placed the right people alongside me throughout the ordeal.

To add further insult to injury, two years later after turning the business around, we had suddenly become a high risk to our bankers, who seemed reluctant to offer us a meaningful overdraft facility, just at the time when we needed it most. Part of our problem was that we were asset-rich, but we had outstanding payments owed to us that amounted to our last five years' profits, a situation that was now seriously affecting our cash flow. This, together with small profit margins, additional overhead costs, and ever-changing expectations from our client base made the situation seem futile. I recall going home one evening, looking at Alison and telling her that I'd had a dreadful experience, where I questioned what I was doing thinking that I could run a company, and that my confidence was totally blown. It was therefore an easy choice to begin preparing the company for sale, but not before market conditions were right for us to sell, and after profit margins and economic conditions had changed for the better.

I was in business for twenty-one years, starting out as a sole trader, and with a £3,000 investment I bought a van, a trailer and some petrol-driven garden equipment. The bulk of my early business came from garden maintenance on vacant properties, repossessed during the 1991 recession. From this market, various other opportunities arose to clean, clear and maintain the properties that I dealt with, and as my confidence grew, I developed the business in to a Limited Company that specialised in insurance building work. Alison and I eventually sold our business in 2012, with an annual turnover of around £850,000.

The new directors talked about offering me a job, utilising my skills in a marketing capacity across their five companies, and I was genuinely excited about the role. It would have fulfilled a genuine passion for a part of the business that I still enjoyed, even though my energy for running a business had subsided and I'd become disillusioned with some clients and the onerous task of managing employees. It was important to us that the existing staff had an option to stay with any new company that purchased us and our attention in ensuring that records, accounts and audits were fully up to date allowed a completion of sale in just six weeks. We were told that this was a record timescale for most business sale transactions. As the new company moved into our offices, a favourable lease was signed and I acted as a consultant for them for another three months, before they eased me out. It was if a big weight had been lifted when, two years later, our original business name was out of circulation, and they moved out of our office premises and relocated all their business back to the Central Midlands area.

During my time setting up and managing our business, it was Alison who had to deal with the outplaying of my frustrations, particularly when I've felt wronged by employees, sub-contractors or clients. She's been the one who's listened to my frustrations, calmed me, encouraged me, or spoken logically about situations, allowing me to see a different perspective on how to actually deal with something. She stepped into the business at crucial times over the years, giving wise counsel, once she sensed that I was ready to listen. I thank God for her and my precious children, for putting up with me during some very stressful times.

Having been taught to save my spending money from a very early age, the belief was that banks or building societies would always be there to support me, if I was wise with my finances. I began to enjoy saving, with an attitude that if I can't afford it, I can't have it. History and experience have taught me that the banks are far from loyal, and during my lifetime I have seen many individuals and businesses ruined, due to greed, selfishness or the bank's lack of wisdom or ruthlessness with their lending policies. I am immensely relieved that even after twenty-one years running our own business, we were never beholden to a lending institution and their fluctuating demands. Instead we adopted a policy that if we needed something, then we saved for it. It was a decision that allowed us an option to consider the enjoyment of an independent lifestyle, from the age of fifty-five years old, mainly due to changes in regulation of private pensions.

Since selling the company in 2012, I've enjoyed raising money for 'The Moldova Charity Mission for the Disabled' by training for and participating in a 170-mile bike ride from Edinburgh to Newcastle, and trekking to Everest base camp with my son, Rory, alongside me. When Rory was sixteen we also served the charity directly in Moldova, by helping disabled children at a summer camp in 2013. A most worthwhile and humbling experience for us both. I now help manage our holiday let in Cornwall, and Alison has been making bespoke Christian jewellery for over ten years. We help Alison's father, Fred, aged ninety-seven, and her step mum, Beryl, aged ninety-three, to retain their independent living, by carrying out regular visits and appropriate chores. In March 2018, I retired (from paid work) after four-and-a-half years, as part-time Manager of a Christian charity, which involved running a community coffee shop in Desborough, Northants. This was a most worthwhile job that allowed me to use most of my skills and ease into full retirement, rather than ending my working life abruptly. What the future holds, I have no idea, but I am excited with our new lifestyle as it offers us flexibility, with lots of time to spend helping our church, meeting up with family, friends and being with each other. I look forward with great anticipation to what God has planned for us in the future, and I hope and pray that writing this book is part of that journey.

As I think of my school motto – 'Mighty Oaks from little acorns grow'- it reminds me what a burdensome logo this could have been if I'd decided to strive and achieve for most of my working life. I'd far rather rely on God's strength, than my own. Better, therefore, to have a biblical motto like John ch15, v.5:

"I am the vine, you are the branches. If you remain in me and I in you, you will bear much fruit; apart from me you can do nothing."

Lord Lewin presenting me with my Navy
Rugby Cap, 1983

Being presented with Flag Officer Flotilla, Proficiency
Award, 1987

Chapter Seven

LOVE IS...?

The Holy Bible is very clear about what 'true love' is, but it took me many years to discover and accept what it said. Previously, I'd determined 'love' to be purely a strong emotional feeling. But what happens when we feel rejected by those that we love, when trust is broken and those strong emotions subside? I've learnt that love is constant, allowing me to forgive, even when I can't always forget, and to accept goodness but reject evil. It's allowed me to honour, respect and devote myself to another person, at different levels in different ways, and at different times in my life, regardless of my circumstances or frame of mind. I now know that God loves you as much as he loves me, and I feel blessed and immensely grateful for discovering what Love is.

Having been brought up with a belief that 'big boys don't cry,' I was able to hold back my tears on 24th August 1976, when my parents waved me off from Sheffield train station, as I left home to begin my journey to Plymouth, to join the Royal Navy. I was a naïve youngster, aged sixteen years and three months, and it was left up to Mum, some years later, to tell me how Dad had reacted when I'd departed – "Your Dad had a tear in his eye and he was very upset, when you left on the train." Initially, I was surprised and taken aback to hear about his response, but as I reflected, it made sense as he had a soft, non-confrontational side to him, only ever losing his temper with me on one occasion when I'd kicked Mum's new copper, waste paper basket whilst in a rage, denting it beyond repair. How things have a tendency to repeat themselves, as I recall doing the very same thing to my daughter, Natasha's, metal waste paper basket after my temper got the better of me, when she was less than eight years old!

To hear that my father was sad about me leaving home was a comfort, a confirmation that he loved and cared for me, even though I'd never heard him say that he did. Emotions were high for most of the recruits, during the first few months after joining up. Unlike myself, many of my new friends, had come from troubled or broken families, and some were keener than others to show misguided loyalty, to those they'd left behind. Tattoos were prevalent, for those old enough to have them, and the biggest and boldest I saw was of a galleon with the words 'The only woman I ever loved was another man's wife, my mum'. Great commitment, until you sober up to the fact that you might one day get married to another woman that you love!

Another friend took great delight in showing me his large portrait of the comic strip character 'Popeye the Sailor,' inked on the inside of a forearm and commissioned after drinking heavily after a night out abroad. Unfortunately, the quality of the artwork was shambolic, proportions out of kilter, and Popeye's trademark pipe was half an inch away from his mouth. He'd had the name DAVID tattooed to the underside of the picture. "Was it your middle name?" I asked. He explained that the only person he could think of called David was a young lad from when he was a nipper, who he used to play out with. "I really loved that lad," Geoff exclaimed!

Some years later, my sister, almost five years younger than me, gave me a very different view of how affectionate my father had been towards her and her children, Natalie and Rebecca. It may have been due to a realisation that he'd missed out on something in our relationship, or more likely that he thought that men shouldn't be tactile with other men, or share their emotions with each other. I eventually saw the same affection, which Julie spoke about, given to our own three children, when he came to visit us, or I would hear it from our girls, when they went to stay with my parents in Sheffield. How often I see or hear of grandparents showing more affection to their grandchildren, than they ever did to their own offspring.

Whether for pleasure, pain, or simply to teach me a lesson, Dad allowed me to take a drag from his half-smoked cigarette when I was ten years old! When he finally gave in to my request, I vigorously inhaled, filling my lungs with smoke that made me gasp for air, cough violently, and make my eyes water. The incident put me off smoking for life, a real blessing as far as I was concerned. On another occasion, some friends came around to my house, after my parents decided to go out to the Working Men's Club to socialise. During the evening I began squashing down the used cigarette butts that had been left in the ash tray, located on a side table. I didn't think much about my actions until Mum returned from her night out and began challenging me about the short butt ends left in a pile in the ashtray. She was teetotal, therefore, totally sober when she began accusing me of having smoked the cigarettes. The following day, and for years to come, she insisted that I'd been smoking on that evening, something that I continually felt hurt about for years afterwards, and it saddened me intensely to know that she didn't believe me.

Both Mum and Dad smoked, and so the smell and passive inhalation of the dense nicotine atmosphere made me gasp for breath. The downstairs rooms of every house we lived in would turn a pale brown colour from the effects of this, and as I grew older, returning back home filled me with dread, as the house had a permanent smell of smoke. I would regularly ask my parents to stop the habit, yet at the same time fuel their temptation with cheap cigarettes that I'd purchased tax-free from the Navy. I believed that I was doing them a favour, saving them money and it was a way to show them loving gratitude for everything they'd done for me. Mum's response was always the same when I pressurised her, claiming that she enjoyed smoking too much to stop, and it was her only vice!

It was such a sad day when in 2002 my loving, affectionate mum was diagnosed with lung cancer, surviving for only two weeks after receiving her test results, aged sixty-seven. A misdiagnosis six months earlier was still enough to make her stop smoking immediately, and the whole family were left speechless at her announcement, as the habit had enticed her for over fifty years. As time went on, the partially collapsed lung was eventually diagnosed as being cancer, and as the symptoms took a hold, the illness became increasingly ruthless. Two days before her death, I arrived on the ward to find her constantly rubbing her leg, mumbling, high on morphine with oxygen, and with plasma drips attached to her body. This was the after-effects of a stroke that had left her paralysed down one side, unable to speak coherently, and in a pitiful, distressing condition.

The realisation that she was helpless and reliant on medical intervention to keep her breathing, created a high degree of physical and emotional tension for all of us there in the room, and I began to question how does all of this end? How long can the doctors mercifully leave someone in this condition, whilst loved ones have to endure the pain of watching a slow and lingering death? I concluded that it's impossible to see the logic in using such extreme intervention to keep people alive, but my father and sister may well have disagreed with me at the time. I have learnt over the years that a line can be crossed when our love for a person can become a selfish desire to hang on to them, for our sake and not necessarily in their best interests. This can sometimes stop the person who's facing death from submitting to the inevitable, creating further anxiety and suffering because they feel that they 'have to fight'. Surely, whenever possible, there has to be dignity in death, and fighting to the last moment isn't always a dignified solution.

It was a welcome relief when Dad agreed to leave Mum's side for an hour or so. It happened to be that my brother-in-law's football team was playing at the local recreation ground, less than a mile away. Hearing laughter, breathing fresh air, and seeing the sun shining was a welcome relief from the sombre atmosphere we'd left behind at the hospital. Garry had been playing in a veterans' league for the over-35s for some time, explaining that there were numerous ex-Sheffield Wednesday players who still had a run-out for his team. It was therefore no surprise to see Chris Waddle (an ex-England international football player) stood in the centre of the pitch verbally dictating play, rather than running fervently up and down the wing, like in his heyday. It was a timely reminder that even the fittest of athletes, eventually slow down as they get older!

As the sadness of Mum's situation unfolded, there was something very special about the affection, closeness and vulnerability shown by all family members, during her last couple of days. For me, I felt closer than ever to her, knowing that her race had been run, and the smile and hug I received from her twelve days previously, reinforced the bond that parents and children sense at special times in their life. It was a time that also drew me ever closer to God, as I sensed great hope about her future, after death, by the peace that I experienced during that time, a unique peace that doesn't make sense in the circumstances. Yes, I challenged God at times, praying earnestly for her recovery, but as my selfishness subsided, I prayed for what was actually best for her and an acceptance of the outcome. To see my father and sister holding on to a hope that Mum would recover or get better, was the epitome of 'love' as they knew it and something I respected. However, as time went by there was a residue of anger aimed at the authorities, when Julie complained against them for their cancer misdiagnosis and other actions relating to Mum's general treatment, and I hope it didn't rob her of being able to grieve properly.

Our reliance and belief that medical intervention should rectify any problem can create an unhealthy and unrealistic level of expectation, particularly when our mortality is in question. We are all beautifully made with a body, soul and spirit that are immensely fragile, and it is well documented that our highly complex bodies can be affected negatively if we mistreat them, whether by diet, habits, or even what we choose to believe. Yet, we readily accept that something mechanical, or a building – in fact, most things – will deteriorate before they should, if poorly maintained or looked after. Most of us at some time have chosen to abuse our bodies, but it seems that over recent years there is a need to be able to 'blame' someone or something, whenever our requirements aren't met, and fuelled by our 'no win, no fee' culture. However, in this instance, and from what I was told, there did seem to be a catalogue of incompetence by some members of the medical profession, and it left my sister immensely frustrated and wanting answers.

Seeing Mum in such distress became intolerable, and it was left for me to ask what could be done about her situation. It was with sympathy and compassion that the doctor advised me that, if the family requested it, they could stop the plasma drip being administered and she would then pass away peacefully. My father eventually acknowledged the decision and it was a relief to see Mum resting in a peaceful and dignified condition before I left to go back home to Kettering, and after the nurse told me that it would be a day or two before Mum would pass away. At home, the next day, I awoke with a start at around 5am, convinced that I'd heard my mum repeatedly shouting my name, and it was an upsetting experience to have such a vivid picture of her in my mind. A little while later I ventured to my workplace office, where I received a call from the hospital to say that she'd passed away peacefully during the night.

I held back tears at Mum's funeral service, after I gave a reading from John ch. 1, where it talks about there being many rooms in heaven, for those who pass away. I later made a point of apologising to our two older children, for not showing any emotion during the time of Mum's passing, reassuring them that I'd broken down several times previously, but mainly at private moments when they weren't around. This proved to be a liberating moment in my life after realising that sometimes there is strength, rather than a weakness, when 'big boys' are able to show their vulnerability.

Mum was a kind person and always made sure I was reminded about family birthdays or other upcoming events. I found her to be the main decision-maker in the household, who dealt with my childhood tantrums the best she could, and as I got older, she would politely let me know if I hadn't called or visited home as often as I should have. One particular time I made a real effort to remember her birthday, sending an unusual card for the occasion and ringing home to wish her a happy birthday. They'd only recently had a telephone installed and she seemed delighted that I'd remembered to send a card on time, explaining how surprised she was. However, what she discovered after opening it was that I'd sent her a Get-Well card, which read 'I thought I'd send you a Get-Well card because by receiving a card on time you'll need to recover, after fainting'. This amused her so much, but at the same time she must have felt exasperated with me, particularly when year after year I missed sending birthday cards out on time. I got better at sending out cards after Alison came into my life. It was always with a sense of affection and some amusement to see how big a card my parents would send to us on our special occasions. I'm sure that there was thoughtfulness and love in their intent but these cards were whoppers, with just a printed one-liner, saying 'Happy something,' and a few written words and kiss symbols added inside. I would joke that the Sheffield market had a lot to answer for, particularly after we began receiving similar-sized cards from my sister as well.

Dad's love for us was reflected mainly through his determination to ensure he was bringing a wage into the household, so that food was always on the table, a breadwinner who was a good, loyal person. There has been great security in knowing that my parents were devoted to each other throughout their marriage, that they were always going to be there for me, something that I knew I would want for my children when I got married. It was only when they were about to leave this world that I sensed how much I really loved them, and realised how much those solid family foundations meant to me.

It was only a matter of months, after Mum died of lung cancer, that Dad began to deteriorate rapidly. Over the next year I made it my mission to tell him that I loved him, as previously mentioning it at the bottom of a card with a couple of kisses had sufficed. One time, we decided to take our three children to see Grandad, for what we thought might be the last time. As we travelled on the M1, northbound from Kettering, I began preparing the rest of the family for what they were about to see.

Natasha, was fourteen, Faith eleven, and Rory was eight and they hadn't seen their grandad for a while. He'd lost several stone in weight over a relatively short period of time, was looking emaciated, and had lost his sense of humour, after suffering from severe depression. His diet seemed to comprise of anti-depressants, sleeping tablets, morphine, and prescription fruit drinks that tasted awful! Seeing his vacant expression gave away his lack of will to go on living, a painful experience to bear for those closest to him. If anyone has ever died of a broken heart it definitely was my father. After the love of his life had passed away and the depression kicked in, it was only a matter of weeks before he was diagnosed with terminal cancer. As conversation dried up, it became increasingly difficult to communicate effectively with him, particularly as he chose to sleep whenever he could.

When my family arrived at his council maisonette in Stannington, on the outskirts of Sheffield, it was lovely to see how the children brought a smile to his face. We all dealt well with the situation throughout the rest of the day, but as we were about to leave, I began to feel nervous about telling Dad that I loved him. The rest of the family said their goodbyes before I took his hand, at the same time saying "You know that we love you." I was slightly tearful, at the same time relieved that I'd fulfilled my promise, but had I? Alison had picked up on me saying that 'we loved him' rather than me telling him that 'I loved him,' and I instantly felt deflated, knowing that I'd bottled out! It was to be some weeks later before I visited and found the courage to tell him directly that I loved him.

It now seems strange, how difficult it was to say those words as a personal statement to my father. But I found it to be a real blessing when I did and thank God for giving me the strength to speak directly from my heart, as I sense that I would have felt guilty for the rest of my life, if I hadn't done so. I could easily tell Mum that I loved her, but just knowing that father and son loved each other, always seemed to be enough. I shall never forget holding my arm around his shoulder, silently praying as we sat on a bench in the grounds of the hospice, just days before he passed away and over two years since his initial cancer diagnosis. He didn't embrace or cuddle me back, saying very little as he snoozed whilst sitting with me in the bright sunny gardens... but that was my dad. We have brought our beautiful children up in an environment where cuddles, kisses, and saying how much we love each other is the norm. We hope we have created a home where respect and compassion for others is taught and I continue to pray that my actions match the loving words that I say to them.

Whilst visiting Dad on an earlier occasion, Rory and I walked from Sheffield train station, through the covered walkways of the bus station, then on towards the city centre, where I'd spotted a young man begging. He had been sitting alone, up against a support pole to one of the walkway canopies. Rory was just seven and it seemed to be an ideal opportunity to try and explain to him about homelessness. For many years, due to my ingrained prejudice, I'd become fearful of engaging with such people, a part of me arguing that they should never have got into the situation they found themselves in, if they had anything about them! I considered them all to be 'dossers,' who were lazy, sponging off others, and that it was their decision to live on the streets.

However, as my Christian faith matured, so I became more aware of Jesus' words that we should love our neighbour as ourselves. My awareness of other people's needs suddenly began to stand out, creating a heartfelt desire to overcome previous prejudices, if the possibility ever arose. Dad had given Rory a Mars to eat, for his journey back home and we waved our goodbyes, before catching the bus back to the train station, talking along the way about how best to help the young homeless man that we'd seen previously. A deal was struck between the two of us that if he was still at the bus station, then Rory was going to offer him the Mars that Grandad had just given to him. As we spotted the guy in the distance, Rory, without hesitation, got so excited that it made my heart race and brought a tear to my eye. My prejudice was still evident as I placed my son between me and the man as some sort of psychological barrier, feeling a real mix of emotions, ranging from excitement to vulnerability to genuine compassion, but at the same time as proud as punch of my lovely son.

We stood over the young man, before he sensed our presence, then he began to slowly raise his hands and head upwards in a motion that suggested he was ready to receive money. Before he could speak, I explained that we wouldn't be giving him any money, but instead began to tell him about my son's generosity of heart, in giving him his present from his very poorly grandad. The guy seemed as pleased and overawed as I was at Rory's kindness, letting out a smile through semi-closed eyes, a smile that betrayed his addiction to something stronger than the chocolate we were giving him. I walked away with a spring in my step, knowing that a massive stronghold was now being dismantled in my soul, at the same time feeling slightly saddened that I'd had to use a child to break down my shameful, ingrained prejudice. I can recall other times when Faith and Natasha's love, kindness and humility have caused me to address some of my personal thoughts, prejudices, and actions over the years. We sometimes spend so much of our time judging others, at the same time oblivious to our own faults, and I think we can learn a lot from a child's innocent but wise council.

I returned home challenged by what had just happened, before promising myself that I would try and help those living on the streets in Kettering. I've always said that actions speak louder than words, and this was another time when I had an opportunity to prove it. I made the decision to meet up at a community coffee shop with a Pastoral Minister, who I knew well, to discuss my thoughts. However, on the way to the meeting I encountered a homeless guy, a situation that could easily have put me off ever wanting to help such a person again. The man was standing directly outside the entrance to the coffee shop that I intended to visit, and he asked me for 50p. The money was supposedly to get his bus fare to go to the next town of Corby, some eight miles away. I thought this was a little strange, as I'd seen him several times before, in the vicinity of the bus station, and knew that the fare cost more than the amount he was asking for. Nevertheless, I built up the courage to engage with him, anticipating that he'd fill me in about his needs, and how tough life was on the streets, before advising me on the best way I could make a real impact on his life.

The reality was that this young man was a professional beggar, a drug addict with very little patience or respect for anyone, and his annoyance at my questioning was clear once he knew that I wasn't going to cross his palm with cash. Entering the coffee shop, I felt disheartened and a little bemused, shocked to know that my compassion had been ignored, but a little warier of what I was letting myself in for. The same man wandered around town most days, sometimes begging, always fidgety or other times walking head down, but with a real purpose! Until, one day after leaving my work-place office to grab some lunch, I noticed him slumped unconscious, possibly dead, in a service area, behind a gate to a large public house. He was being treated by paramedics, and I never saw him on the streets of Kettering again.

Challenged by what I'd seen, it was a few days later that I discovered that the town had a drop-in centre, so I popped in to enquire about how best I could help them, if at all. One of the managers, George, seemed to be pleased that I'd come to see them and told me about how they were in the process of creating a committee to expand the awareness of the homeless dilemma, that was developing in and around the Kettering area. I was advised that the problems were immense, but that the real issue was convincing the Council to support the project. I immediately found myself making a mental note of the many things that I felt I could offer, then signed up to be part of the team.

It wasn't long before I'd found additional volunteers to help at the centre, struck a deal with Marks and Spencer to supply some food, and created a voucher scheme to sell to establishments, that they could then pass on to the homeless to use at the drop-in. I met with a councillor to discuss the prospects of purchasing a building to offer overnight accommodation, but costs and regulations proved too big an obstacle to overcome. The problems mounted as I began to understand more about the difficulties surrounding the actual definition of 'homeless', and how few of them wanted the help that we and the Council could provide. Nevertheless, I prayed about the situation and decided to persevere and support the project the best I could, taking time to speak with several of the homeless, at their pitches, during my lunchtime breaks.

One of the first people I introduced to the centre was a dishevelled man, who was begging outside Marks and Spencer, and I began the conversation with 'Hello, I know it's obvious that you need help, but are you aware that there's a drop-in centre down the road?' He politely informed me that he didn't need help, that he was happy living in his car, travelling the country with his best friend who was a dog, and that this had been his lifestyle for the last eleven years. What did enthuse him about the centre, once I'd made my apologies to him for my presumptions, was that he could engage with like-minded people, to while away the daytime hours in the comfort of a warm building. It was encouraging to see him thereafter, regularly attending the drop-in centre. I learnt a valuable lesson from this experience, in never assuming that anything's obvious, and became more aware of the pitfalls of doing so.

There was a temptation to approach another guy, but I avoided him for some reason, even though he dressed poorly, looked dirty, and was found begging each day outside the NatWest Bank. He seemed happy enough, played his guitar, and engaged amicably with many people as they handed over their loose change. One day, I spotted a friend chatting to him and decided that I'd hang around to see if he knew anything about the homeless guy's situation. It transpired that the man came in each morning from a surrounding town, parked up his estate car for the day, changed into dirty clothing, then played his instrument outside the bank until he'd cleared £100 in cash, which was generally by 1pm. This person was clearly abusing the general public's generosity by doing what he did, and to hear about such things can easily put many people off helping those genuine in need.

However, I continued helping out at the centre, but began asking more questions and became more discerning about my involvement there. It's a good and honourable thing to be able to offer loving kindness to those who require it, rather than doing nothing at all, but kindness is also something that many homeless people can become immune to, particularly if they are supporting an addiction. Putting boundaries in place, still allowed me to be an advocate of supporting the homeless, with gestures of food, service, conversation, and goodwill, over and above giving them cash, the exception being if they were selling The Big Issue magazine.

To celebrate the committee's formation and highlight the problems of homelessness, the drop-in centre managers organised a social. Alison, came along with me to the BBQ and we sat next to a lady who was originally from Liverpool, who had a sad tale to tell, and proceeded to tell us about how she'd let her family down time after time through her addictions. The woman was slight, in her mid-forties, with a scarred, wrinkled, leathery face, features that portrayed a long history of severe hardship and abuse. She'd clearly made an effort with her appearance, wearing makeup and tying back her hair to show off her pretty chiselled, facial features. As far as I could make out, she was sober, showing a real desire to be reunited with her daughter, which she said was now in a process of reconciliation. It seemed to be a real good news story, something that lifted the heart and further motivated me, when suddenly a young man sat next to us and immediately distracted the woman's attention away from our conversation. This was privately appreciated by me as it gave an opportunity to savour the delights of the BBQ, rather than constantly wrestling with my temptations, after smelling the lovely food for over half an hour! The man had brought a plastic bag with him, which I later discovered had an unlabelled bottle of clear liquid inside. I never saw the lady take a drink from the bottle but within minutes she changed, becoming totally fixated on the young man, yet oblivious to Alison and I. It was noticeable because of the speed at which her personality changed from being lucid, articulated and warm, to suddenly becoming intoxicated, a change that affected her whole demeanour.

After leaving the social a short while later, I made a point of regularly enquiring about the woman's wellbeing. She was well-known to the managers, someone who sofa-surfed, a person who generally had no fixed abode but relied on friends to put her up overnight. As well as being an alcoholic, she had a drug addiction and no chance of seeing her family members anytime soon, and what she'd told us about a possible reconciliation with her daughter was a lie. A few months later there was an enquiry into her death, after she was found in a local terraced house, having fallen down some stairs. How much loving care can you give to a person who is intent on self-destruction, probably never enough? People need to have a desire to change themselves for it to be of any real benefit, but providing our motives are right, it shouldn't stop us from making ourselves available to them, giving them hope and encouragement by showing that somebody cares.

I made time to regularly converse with two young men, when I discovered that they were homeless and addicted to drugs. They'd become friends during their travels and had been introduced to the drop-in centre previously, but dismissed the idea of using the services, and that saddened me. Eventually, one made the effort to seek out rehabilitation through a Christian organisation in Wales, and managed to move back home to live with his sister in Plymouth – a real success story. The other chap, initially a man who seemed emotionally stronger than his colleague, struggled with attempts at making any impression when he attempted rehabilitation, something he admitted to me was a regular failing. One of my last conversations with him was when he told me that he'd had enough of 'this crap' and needed to sort himself out and get back to Manchester, where his family lived. I hope he made it, on both counts.

My association with the centre ended one year later when the two paid managers left their job, both at the same time and quite abruptly, offering no explanation. I later found out that the Housing Association and YMCA couldn't seem to strike a deal to prolong the lease on the building or offer an alternative solution, and I can only assume that funding for the managers' positions was being cut. My impression was that if you took the effort or had the ability to register as homeless, with local authorities or relevant agencies, then help and assistance was available to you, and it was something the drop-in centre would actively help with. However, there were still gaps in the system that weren't easy to reconcile, and it was a concern to see the amount of people using our facilities or wandering the streets who refused to sign up for benefits or seek long-term help. As a structured and pragmatic person, myself, I fought the temptation to become judgemental, accepting that society as we know it had become too much for them, for whatever reason, but from time to time I reminded myself to be careful, as some attendees may have been hiding from the authorities! Sometimes, their excuses to live on the streets aren't always logical, and the longer people stay registered as homeless, their motives become even more blurred, leading to spiralling and uncontrollable behaviour that generally results in feeding a habit. It seems that when a person chooses to buck the trend in our society, it is easier for them to fall into a void that can rapidly create a sense of despair, if intervention isn't sought or offered early enough. The end results can be catastrophic, and I do believe that but by the grace of God, the next homeless person could be you or I.

Several churches have since stepped in to keep the drop-in centre functioning, when it seemed certain that it would close, and it was sometime later when a meeting was held to discuss the way ahead. After lots of talk about procedures and budgets, I was able to nervously express my own views. After representatives from the Council, Social Services, Accommodation Concern and YMCA had debated issues purely from a business viewpoint. I felt that the church representation had been totally overlooked. I pointed out that without the voluntary work of church members, who were now heavily involved at the centre, the drop-in wouldn't be in existence, no matter what was agreed. I said that from time to time, we need the freedom to show compassion, that we should be able to pray with the needy and place a loving arm around them, when circumstances allow it or an individual requests it. I stated that the real challenge was not if the churches could work with them, but whether they were willing to work with us, comments that brought the assembly to silence and without any response, as the meeting came to a close. I can only imagine what was going through people's minds regarding safeguarding, health and safety, and other politically correct procedures, but I was later thanked by several church ministers and leaders for my comments. It is at our peril we forget that 'love conquers all,' and overcoming ingrained prejudice, allowed me to find compassion far beyond what I thought I was capable of showing.

Love for some people means spoiling their pets; personally I have only ever had one dog in my lifetime, which was a poodle crossed with something else. What the something else was, I'm still unsure about, but the dog was given to us as a puppy by Nan Wood when I was eleven years old. A kind and loving action in itself, but my parents were totally unaware of the gift until it was dropped into my arms, early one morning. The white, curly, fluff-ball was an instant heart-melter, and the perfect present for any youngster. I can only assume that the gesture was done for all the right, loving reasons, but definitely lacked wise discernment from my Nan. Looking after animals is a big task, taking a huge commitment of time and energy, and one that comes with a price tag that I'm convinced my parents weren't ready for. Unfortunately, many years later, Mum felt that Nan had been too much of an overbearing influence, throughout most of her married life, and eventually broke off all communication with her. Dumping the dog into my arms must surely have been one of those moments that did irreparable damage to their relationship.

We named the dog Queenie, but it didn't really reflect her character, particularly as she got older. We were now living in a private semi-detached house built on a steep road, which by design gave us a small rear garden, and the flat-roofed carport quickly became part of the dog's territory! Queenie was overweight, but if she heard people passing by, became adept at running from the back garden, jumping on to the flat roof of the car port, before sliding within inches of the front edge, some eight feet above the pavement. Our cuddly cross-bred, poodle became a snarling beast and scared the living daylights out of any unsuspecting passers-by, but I was still able to feel a deep affection for the dog, even though she attempted to bite anyone, except family members, who tried to access the property.

I would sometimes take her to see Nan, whose house was now just over a mile away, most of the journey being uphill. Unfortunately, the dog was so unfit that after walking no more than 10 metres, she would stop dead still, to the point that I would have to drag her along by her lead. Eventually, I would be forced to carry her for the rest of the journey tucked away under my anorak coat. Queenie's head would pop out above the coat's zip at chest height, and at times like this I felt a deep love for the pet.

I've never felt the urge to own a dog since that time and I would often joke that I might consider owning one, if it was accompanied with veg, gravy or a curry sauce. This negative attitude probably came about when my friend, Simon, dumped his Springer Spaniel on me when I lived near the seafront at Weymouth, and based at the nearby naval air base. He left me with no choice as he slammed the door shut behind him saying 'See ya, back in a week's time, Glyn!' To say that the dog was a menace was an understatement, as it ate anything and everything that was left any lower than the height of a mantlepiece, including a family tub of margarine. Following which it left a trail of vomit and diarrhoea throughout the three-storey house. To add insult to injury, on the first morning walk along the beach I noted several well-behaved pooches off their lead, running back and forth or chasing tennis balls. How pleasant I thought, until the Springer disappeared into the distance, running ever further away the nearer I got to him! I arrived at work almost an hour late after missing my bus and sweating like a pig.

But, my view of dogs has since changed after 'Ronnie Wood' came into my life in 2018. Not only did Natasha, move back in with us after working away for two years, but we inherited a Cockapoo called Ronnie. Suddenly, without warning, I found myself handing out treats regularly, walking him like I've never walked before, and talking to him, even when no-one was around! I even allow him to eat veg, gravy and curry sauce when no-one's looking!

At just five years old I remember having a 'gushy feeling' for a girl called Julie, when she spoke to me at the school gates. She seemed nice, but lost me when she said that she'd got lots of boyfriends. There were several other girls that I felt 'gushy' about as I made my way through junior, then comprehensive school, but due to my shyness, I didn't really get to know any of them. However, they always seemed to be the best-looking girls in the school, who I viewed from afar and were always out of my league. Jade was someone I became infatuated with for the longest period of time, spanning some ten years. I'd spotted her as an eight-year-old, admiring her looks before taking the time to try and catch her attention. I must have received a glimpse back from her at some time, but I misinterpreted this as my opportunity to let her friends know that I liked her and from that moment on she avoided me, making it clear that she wasn't interested. My bravest moment was giving her a Love Heart sweet, which said something like 'I love you', when I was still at junior school. Most boys seemed content with having 'friends, who were girls' or none at all, whereas I wanted a girl that was going to be my best friend.

As I got older my feelings for Jade subsided, then grew again, as I came across her at different times of my life. Once my parents' moved house and happened to be only a hundred metres from her family home. Between the age of seventeen and eighteen, I was so keen on her, that I felt like I would be letting her down if she ever found out that I was chasing after other girls! I knew that she'd already broken up with a good friend of mine a year earlier, because he was leaving Sheffield to join the Royal Navy, and I should have realised then that I stood no chance of having any sort of relationship with her, because I was already serving in the Navy! Nevertheless, I was determined to ask her out whilst home on leave, but I was as nervous as could be as she passed by my parents' lounge window. Walking towards the bus stop I eventually caught her up, but I was left gasping for breath after running up the steep hill, before summoning the courage to ask "Would you like to go out for a drink sometime?" Her reply was considerate, kind, but the wrong one for me, as she'd begun dating someone else, who she later got engaged to. I returned home despondent, realising that my affections for her weren't ever going to be reciprocated.

I'd been brought up in a stable, happy family where marriage was accepted as a lifelong commitment, but sub-consciously, I believe that I was searching for a wife, based on emotions that were impossible to fulfil. I wanted someone who I could totally trust, accepting me for who I was, but it was based on an assumption that they were perfect, without me really knowing them, the result being that I found myself feeling let down by girls, even though I barely knew them! How long any of these relationships would have really lasted, if they'd been allowed to develop, I'll never know because none of them ever came about. I did start seeing girls from the age of fifteen, all of which were pretty innocent experiences, but exciting at times.

I was now eighteen, still looking for 'Miss Right', when one of the WRENS (Women of the Royal Naval Services) took an interest in me, after I'd returned back to my parent station at RNAS Yeovilton, having just completed my first stint on the Field Gun Crew. Feeling free to find my next potential bride, but as naive as ever, I found that women were becoming quite flirty with me, but for all the wrong reasons. I was six-feet-two, weighed in at well over fifteen stones, not having an ounce of fat on me, with a macho reputation that preceded me wherever I went. The reality was that I was still shy with women, unless I'd had a drink, and I lacked confidence in most things, other than playing sport.

The WREN was older than me and engaged to be married, making me think that she must be really keen, if she's ready to leave her fiancé! I became interested in her, then began meeting up, generally after a few drinks at the regular NAAFI discos. She thought that I was wasting my time, waiting for the 'love of my life' to come along, and made it clear that she'd never leave her partner for anyone, which came as a bit of a shock! Her advice was to go home on leave, get off with someone that I had no feelings for, then come back to take advantage of the many girls that were on offer, including her! I did just that, losing my virginity to a girl in Sheffield, who I tried to get to like but had very little respect for, before ending the relationship by phone after a few weeks. I persevered with dating for a little while longer, my longest relationship lasting just six months, before I received my first posting to a ship which I used as my excuse to walk away from the friendship. The reality was that I was looking forward to my new-found freedom to engage in as many physical relationships as possible, my restlessness evident, the more I tried to settle down or deal with girls' feelings. I knew that I wouldn't and couldn't be unfaithful and my moral values would not have allowed me to have cheated on a 'girlfriend,' prompting me to vow that if I ever got serious, I'd always remain loyal to them. Until that moment I began to make up for what I considered to be lost time, but I now acknowledge that some girls felt hurt during this period, and I apologise for that.

I still had a weakness to become infatuated and I fell for a girl some years later, after an intermittent chase that lasted two years. I instantly stopped messing about, once I thought we were dating, but it proved a torrid time and probably some payback for what I'd put some girls through previously. A turning point occurred when she flippantly told me to, "go and find someone else to marry!" I was shocked to hear such a response as there was no way that I was ready for marriage, even though I was so besotted and, sometimes overwhelmed with jealousy towards her. I eventually realised that I'd built up this young woman into something she never was, and my mistake was to place her on a pedestal without really getting to know her properly. This allowed my pride to get the better of me, at the same time exposing a perceived weakness and vulnerable side to my personality, which I disliked intensely! The emotional rollercoaster made me feel very uncomfortable, and I began to seriously question what sort of relationships I wanted in future, at a time when I'd begun travelling to play for Northampton Saints at the weekends.

I was kindly put up at Simon's house in Kettering, just twenty miles away from Northampton, where I socialised with a group that included members of Kettering Rugby Club and their partners, one of whom was called Alison. She was dating an old friend of mine and it soon became apparent what a lovely person she was, when I found myself opening up to her about my recent relationship issues in Weymouth. I'd never really spoken to anyone so openly before, finding it therapeutic and trusting that the information given would go no further. We got on incredibly well, although I seemed to get on well with most people, but initially there were no deep emotional or overwhelming feelings for her. For several months, when our paths crossed, we spoke as friends about everyday things and probably even about the weather!

I held back from getting too close and it was some months later that Alison broke up with her boyfriend after he disclosed that he wanted a more permanent relationship, something she didn't feel was right for her. She still came out for drinks with her friends, and I could sense that our friendship was developing, although I was still living a very different lifestyle in Weymouth, to the one that I was displaying in Kettering. However, I found a freedom that allowed me to be myself and relaxed in Alison's company, that gradually developed into respecting and trusting her implicitly, to the point where I began to look out for her at every opportunity. Most of the people that I met in Kettering were in long-standing relationships, implying that perhaps I'd got it wrong, that to have a partner was more about friendship, which can grow over a period of time, rather than relying on the intense, instant, physical and emotional feelings that I'd reacted to for most of my life. I deliberated about asking her out, but before doing so I knew that I had to give up the promiscuous lifestyle that I was still enjoying many miles away in Weymouth.

Our first meeting together, independent of others, was in August 1984 on a weekend when Alison was flying out to Texas to meet her close friend, Jean, for a once-in-a-lifetime holiday. I was performing in the Royal Tournament at Earl's Court, London, in the Field Gun Competition for the third time, and she'd mentioned that she'd like to come and see the event, before departing from Heathrow Airport. Afterwards, we had a nice meal at Covent Garden, meeting again on the Sunday at Hyde Park, but unfortunately, my insecurity and independence got the better of me as she was about to leave. Instead of booking another date on her return, I said that if she was ever passing through Weymouth at any time, to pop in and see me! Apparently, that went down like a lead balloon, and she departed to the USA, thinking that there was no chance of ever having a relationship with me, quite disillusioned, but looking forward to finding a nice American man, rather than wasting her time over me.

By the time Alison returned from the States, several weeks later, the rugby season had started again. I was staying at my friend's house in Kettering, still playing for 'the Saints', but with a realisation that I'd missed my beautiful girl friend, whilst she'd been away. It was therefore an easy option to ring her at her parents' house to ask if she'd like to go out for a drink. Within a few weeks our relationship was out in the open, which seemed to please many, but although we never sensed any hostility towards us, it disappointed some, as her ex was well liked.

I'd spent several weeks distancing myself from female acquaintances in Weymouth, as I knew the moment Alison left for the USA, that I wanted to be committed to her. As our relationship developed, I realised that I'd never allowed myself the time or had the opportunity to grow close or trust a girl, based on their personality. It was still a while before I eventually fell in love with Alison's tender, gentle, kind and patient ways, and at times, early on in our relationship, I still felt confused about how I was really feeling. Our trusting, long-distance relationship lasted for almost two years, before I proposed to Alison, one damp October evening at a romantic spot in the Nothe Gardens located in the old harbour of Weymouth. As we reached the softly lit waterfall, that had been built to celebrate the recent wedding of Prince Charles to Princess Diana, I thought it was the perfect setting to ask Alison to marry me. It was both a relief and beautiful experience when she said 'Yes' to my proposal.

I was now on a journey that allowed me to discover what I believed true love to be, a journey where the importance and relevance of marriage only became truly apparent when I accepted the Christian faith, at the age of thirty-seven. When we enter into marriage, as described and prescribed by scripture, there is a spiritual bond with our partner that is both pleasing and blessed by God, and the verses in 1 Corinthians. ch.13 made a mockery of my misguided notion of what I thought love should be:

If I speak in the tongues of men or of angels, but do not have love, I am only a resounding gong or a clanging cymbal. If I have the gift of prophecy and can fathom all mysteries and all knowledge, and if I have a faith that can move mountains, but do not have love, I am nothing. If I give all I possess to the poor and give over my body to hardship that I may boast, but do not have love, I gain nothing.

Love is patient, love is kind. It does not envy, it does not boast, it is not proud. It does not dishonour others, it is not self-seeking, it is not easily angered, it keeps no record of wrongs. Love does not delight in evil but rejoices with the truth. It always protects, always trusts, always hopes, always perseveres.

Love never fails. But where there are prophecies, they will cease; where there are tongues, they will be stilled; where there is knowledge, it will pass away. For we know in part and we prophesy in part, but when completeness comes, what is in part disappears. When I was a child, I talked like a child, I thought like a child, I reasoned like a child. When I became a man, I put the ways of childhood behind me. For now we see only a reflection as in a mirror; then we shall see face to face. Now I know in part; then I shall know fully, even as I am fully known.

And now these three remain: faith, hope and love. But the greatest of these is love.

Sometime during 2011, a very close and dear friend sent me a text, something I wouldn't normally have picked up on until a long while later in the day. I'd decided to work from home this particular morning with the mobile phone by my side, when the message came through telling me that he'd had enough of life, was ending it, and how much he valued and loved me for my friendship. The suicide text was confirmation of something that he'd talked about for a long time, after facing financial ruin from the economic collapse in 2008 and suffering with dreadful health problems from his time serving in the army in the first Gulf War in 1991. I was able to leave the house immediately, after asking Alison to raise the alarm with the emergency services, and I sped over to see him some twenty miles away, fearing the worst. He'd written out personal letters to his wife, two children, myself and a family friend, and all were neatly arranged around the fireplace when I arrived. The ambulance services had reached him just a few minutes earlier, after he'd drunk half the cocktail of prescription drugs and alcohol that he'd made up. The remainder sat in a large glass on the fire hearth, and his first words to me when I entered the living room were "What are you doing here?"

I stayed with him for several hours in the A+E department of the town hospital, chatting through how he'd got to this point, and whether it was a serious attempt to take his life or a cry for help. I knew things were bad, but he is proud, sometimes a stubborn man who has been brought up to ensure he supports his family and be the head of the household, and when that began to crumble, so did he. His unwillingness to accept support and the fact he was suffering from depression, but chose not to accept the diagnosis, didn't help matters, but my love and concern for him allowed me to show empathy and give time and advice, whenever I could.

Since that time, he's been treated for clinical depression, diagnosed with an incurable disease, and was given a year to live in 2013, but is still alive today, which seems to be a miracle as far as I'm concerned. For a majority of the time, up until now, communication has mainly been from my end, but I pray regularly for him, his family and hope that he retains his faith, how little he regards that to be. When we do meet it's like we've never been apart and our friendship seems to blossom again, with promises made about keeping in touch but which are difficult to fulfil, mainly because he spends a majority of his time living abroad.

There's a beautiful verse in Proverbs (ch.18, v.24) that reads,

'A man of many companions may come to ruin, but there is a friend who sticks closer than a brother.'

So far, I have only sensed that love and closeness for another man on three occasions in my life. It's what I still sense for this friend but I have to admit that I sometimes feel disheartened when at times, it seems a one-sided friendship. But I mention this story because whatever I think or feel, however frustrated I get, I'm reminded that my God is a God of pure, unadulterated love who never changes or gives up on anybody. That means accepting that my God loves you as much as he loves me, whoever you are and whatever you've done; it's just our sin that he hates...and we're all guilty of that!

Therefore, I choose to keep in contact with my friend, accepting our friendship for what it is, using God's strength, rather than my own, to maintain the bond that we have. Because I've sampled God's love and the freedom that brings, through what Jesus did on the cross for me, it's made sharing my love with others that much easier, and it's a free gift that anyone can receive, we just need to believe and ask for it.

Mum, Glyn and Julie together with our beast of a dog, Queenie

Precious times reading a story with Natasha and Faith

Glyn's Mum and Dad in good health before their cancer diagnosis

Alison with our beautiful daughters, Natasha and Faith, 1995

Rory, with his first pet - a Guinea pig called Snowy

Moldova Charity Mission For The Disabled holiday club team, 2013
Glyn, back row, far left; Rory, front row, far left

Chapter Eight

MY LORD AND MY GOD

Thomas, a young man, best remembered as 'Doubting Thomas' and a disciple of Jesus Christ, was transformed when he met with the risen Lord and was the first person to be recorded as saying the words; 'My Lord and My God.' How fortunate for Thomas that he was given a second chance to meet with the risen Jesus, to fulfil his request to see the cruel marks of torture and death on Jesus' body, before he'd believe that the resurrection had taken place. How unfortunate for Thomas that he would be persecuted for the rest of his life, as he proclaimed 'The Good News' about Jesus Christ, Our Living God.' This is my story of how I came to declare that Jesus is 'My Lord and My God.'

For years I wasn't sure about who this Jesus was, but I assumed that there was 'a God.' I felt that I had high moral values, but found it easy to ignore those values when circumstances suited me, and I sometimes felt like a hypocrite. It now gives me immense hope to know that someone who walked, talked and touched Jesus was still sceptical, even after seeing the incredible work and miracles that Jesus carried out. It means that when we doubt or mess up, we can still say sorry for our lack of faith, knowing that our God still loves us and wants to have a personal relationship, but based on grace (undeserved love) and forgiveness. After the execution of Jesus it seems that history has judged Thomas as a doubter, but who could have blamed him? His faith and trust in Jesus, the Messiah who'd come to save him, was now being challenged. Even as those within the inner circle were announcing that Jesus had been resurrected and, they'd seen and spoken to him, Thomas proclaimed that, "unless I see the marks on his hands and feet, I will not believe."

I'm often asked what the crisis was when I turned to Christ. In other words, no normal person would turn to Christianity unless they were desperate. My response would be 'crisis, what crisis!' However, I would partially agree, that it is during difficult times or when we are at our most vulnerable, when we are more likely to hear God's gentle call, and particularly if we are used to relying on our own strength to deal with situations. My conversion was more a realisation that there's got to be something more fulfilling than what I'd previously relied on during my lifetime. It was then that I began to swallow my pride, allowing me to begin a journey to investigate the Christian faith.

As a young boy I remember a passionate story of how Nan had survived a traumatic experience whilst giving birth. "You must always pray!" she exclaimed as she proceeded to tell me how she'd avoided death, whilst giving birth to her son, my father, Keith. There were severe complications with the birth, causing her to lose a great deal of blood, whilst enduring dreadful pain. 'I was praying, when He came and held my hand.' Nan told the story as though this person, Jesus Christ, was there in the room with her. She went on to explain how she'd had a tangible experience of Jesus holding her hand, when she was at her most vulnerable. Another time Nan had taken me to see Kitty and Mary, two of her old friends, who lived like female versions of Steptoe and Son, the television characters from the 70s. The sisters were lovely people who lived in cramped, dirty conditions, hoarding items from bygone years throughout their property. On the way back from their house we got off the bus to walk over the Bole Hills, which consisted of a series of steep grassy banks that had been sculptured into a large parkland, from a quarried site. We stopped, then looking at the view before us, with the wind blowing into our faces, she commented on how God had created everything, encouraging me to close my eyes, and then prompted me to clasp my hands together and pray. I felt most awkward as I listened intently for God to talk back to me, before eventually succumbing to my lack of patience and concentration, not quite sure how to end the time of prayer until Nan broke the silence.

Through compulsory Religious Education classes at school, I had a vague understanding of who Jesus was, but I can't ever recall thinking that the person who Nan had spoken about, was the same person I was being taught about! I began to go to church at the age of ten, as a consequence of being a member of the local Cubs group, something I did only because some of my friends had joined. However, I found church to be extremely boring, with Sunday School ever so tedious and my abiding memory was of a small wooden board, with several different numbers on, each relating to a song in our hymn book. There were at least five hymns to get through each week but at some stage the children would be taken into a hall, which was the setting for Sunday school, then expected to listen to Bible stories and draw pictures associated with the parables.

One particular Sunday a child scribbled on my drawing after it had been placed on the floor, ready for viewing by the teachers. I was so infuriated that I stamped all over the girl's picture, as my form of retribution, before being grabbed by a lady who shook me vigorously. After telling me what a horrible boy I was, I meekly accepted the rebuke with a tear in my eye and begrudgingly apologised to the girl. However, I felt a strong sense of injustice that the other child had got away lightly, and it was to be many years later, before I embraced Christ's teaching of turning the other cheek!

Attendance at church involved dressing up in my smartest clothes and shoes, but I felt uncomfortable doing so, mainly because there was always a gang of boys, all older than me, congregating near my house. The thought that they were ridiculing me made the embarrassment almost overwhelming, after being dropped off home and enduring the short walk across a road to my front door. Neither Pete nor his friends ever said anything to indicate that they were ever thinking ill of me, although the looks and stares were enough to make me think otherwise. Also, to be thought of as a soppy, church-going boy was tough to endure, and after a few weeks attending Cubs, where I was expected to wear a neckerchief, talk to someone called Akela, and say 'dib, dib, dib,' with a promise to do my best, was a step too far and I knew that I'd had enough. Reciting a pledge in front of the rest of the group proved nerve-wracking, even though I had been word perfect, practising in private, at home. It was therefore a relief to step back from the mundane rituals and commitments of attending the group and church.

About this time, my peer group, that I considered to be my closest friends, seemed to distance themselves, and I recall feeling hurt when they established a 'special meeting place,' down the side of Henry's garage for best friends only, but this wasn't a get-together that I was invited to. Even though my friend only lived two doors away in an established 1930s semi-detached house, the cultural differences between us were immense, as his father was a headmaster and expectations of Henry were always high. Playing out was my most enjoyable pastime and I began making new friends, most of whom lived further afield, but who tended to be quieter individuals. However, meeting up with a lad who was a genuine loner proved to be a big mistake, and it soon became apparent that he was a bit messed up! We were play-fighting in a field one time when he managed to get his knees either side of my head, pinned my shoulders to the ground, and then produced a knife that he held against my cheek, before telling me what he could do to me. I began to make more effort with my old friends again after this incident, but none of the friendships developed closely, they were just convenient.

At comprehensive school, Religious Education lessons were compulsory and taught by the deputy headmaster, Mr Wardle. He was the strictest teacher in school, took no prisoners, and always expected a quiet classroom within seconds of his lesson starting. It was never a study that I enjoyed or looked forward to, as it seemed irrelevant. The stories were taught in such a way that they seemed to have no real historical or spiritual dimension, making it a very tedious subject. With History being one of my favourite lessons, I may have taken more interest if it had been further explained how the sixty-six books of the Bible were written by forty different authors over a long period of time, and the historical provenance of the literature expanded upon! Most importantly, the real significance of Jesus' death, resurrection and a better understanding of the Holy Spirit were never taught! Like most families, we celebrated Easter with chocolate eggs and Christmas with presents, avoiding the religious aspect of the occasions. A clear case of the secular taking over the sacred, right under my nose, but without even knowing or realising it! With faith playing a very small part in my life, I was left to develop my character based on good family principles, and so long as I wasn't naughty and no one got hurt, things were fine!

It was the school holidays, and a group of us had gathered in the dining room of our new house in Fern Road to play a game called Ouija. It wasn't long before we were all struck with fear and began leaping out of our seats, as the small glass moved around a board, seemingly unaided and spelling out answers to our questions! This is now something I would strongly advise against as it encourages communication with spirits. Even though my mum played down the experience and made light of it, we all thought it best to stop playing the game a short time later. This event, further added to my conviction that there is a spiritual dimension to life, but not always one that is good or beneficial to us. No-one ever owned up to applying additional pressure to the glass on the Ouija board; in fact, at one time we all eased off, to prove to each other that it was moving by itself and we all left the room mystified, with no plans to play the game ever again.

My parents never showed any interest in 'religion,' but I discovered some years later that my mum's mother had been a devout Christian, passing away when Mum was just eight years old. Both my parents told me that they were expected to go to church as youngsters, resulting in them being confirmed in their teenage years, but both eventually turning their backs on church when they were old enough to do so. However, they openly admitted that their faith, or lack of it, was due to Mum feeling let down by God after losing her mother at such an early age. Another obstacle was Mum having to deal with the sorrow of losing a son, Paul, who was stillborn. It seems that many people of their generation and before were left by themselves, to work through the aftermath of personal trauma or disaster and it's perhaps one of the reasons why church attendance has dropped substantially since the First World War.

Another religious encounter occurred when I was eleven years old, whilst playing at a friend's house. His older sister bounded in to the living room and proclaimed that we could all go to heaven when we died, but only if we said 'Yes to Jesus Christ!' The four of us were asked to sit at a table, then directed to close our eyes, whilst repeating some words that she said was a prayer of commitment.

Our sniggering gradually subsided when we all clasped our hands together ready to pray, and before we knew it, she'd jumped up and announced that we were all saved and now Christians! Unfortunately, although keen to show her love of Jesus at the time, she eventually turned her back on her faith; a sad loss, but a warning that the world is ready to swallow us up if our faith is shallow and our teaching inconsequential.

Three years later I joined a youth club with a Christian ethos, called Pathfinders, but it was after being convinced that playing five-a-side football on Friday evenings was a good idea, rather than for any religious reasons. I'd also taken a shine to a girl called Debbie, who attended the club most weeks to play table tennis, but the downside was that you had to attend church at least once a month, to retain your affiliation! The thought of playing footie and the possibility of having my first girlfriend, overcame any previous reservations about the Christian faith, although there was bible teaching for those who sought it. However, at some point, my attention turned back to wanting to know more about God! The message being taught by the leaders was that, firstly, we should read part of the Bible each day; secondly, that we should pray each day; and thirdly, that we attend church once a week. I fell well short of doing these three ritualistic things, but my zeal to tell my family how they could ensure they were all heaven-bound, led Mum and Dad to question what I'd joined up to. My parents became so convinced that the club was some sort of sect or cult, that they requested a meeting with the leaders to allay their fears. Their concerns were unfounded as it turned out, when it was explained to them that the youth club was a Church of England group, led by my History teacher, and that I'd been overzealous in my misguided interpretation of the gospel. Perhaps the emotional pain from Grandad's death, when I was left wondering if he was in heaven or not, was still influencing me, or it could have been my first encounter of the Holy Spirit?

As a result of these experiences and up until my late teens, I still held a reverence for a God, but without fully understanding the link between Jesus Christ, Father God and the Holy Spirit. But, as temptations and worldly pleasures took hold, religion became less important and irrelevant, creating a selfish, independent and irreverent person that just wanted a good time and to be happy!

Many years later, when I'd been married for a few years, a hearse pulled up directly outside our house, after a nearby neighbour's wife lost her battle with cancer. As members of the Salvation Army, most of the neighbour's family, dressed in their uniform, were collected from the house. After seeing the husband and some of the close relations joyfully smiling, it made me feel very uneasy. I'd purposely avoided talking to our neighbour for a long period of time, after his wife, had been given a terminal diagnosis and become bedridden. I felt embarrassed and totally inept in dealing with the emotions of people who were trying to cope with such issues, and I did my best to avoid my neighbour during this time, and for many months afterwards.

It was several more years and after my conversion to the Christian faith, before I was able to accept and understand that a funeral should be a celebration of life, even though there is still sorrow and grief intertwined in the occasion. It is a wonderful place to be, when our faith is secure enough to know that death isn't the end and the best is yet to come. This difficult situation helped me to stay close to, rather than hide from, another neighbour, when she was diagnosed with terminal cancer a few years later. Later on, I dealt far better with my own parents' battles with the illness, even though none had accepted Christ as their Saviour, as far as I knew. I believe that we can all learn to care, it's just a case of how far we're prepared to go in doing so, and these sad experiences have allowed me to have more empathy for those who I encounter in similar circumstances.

Having just retired from playing rugby as captain of Bedford, aged thirty, I'd taken up a voluntary position at Kettering as the forwards' coach. Our family business was still in its infancy, and we'd celebrated the birth of Natasha some months earlier. Saturday nights out with the rugby lads became a regular thing, and generally I would have too many beers, and then finish off the evening with a spicy curry, before getting home well after midnight. Life was good, the business was building up nicely, and at the same time I was enjoying some success with coaching the rugby team. However, from nowhere, Alison mentioned that we should perhaps consider having Natasha christened, but I didn't realise that she meant we should both start attending the Sunday morning service at our local parish church, within a matter of weeks!

I reluctantly agreed and began attending church intermittently, sometimes hungover and smelling of curry from the night before, convinced that most people still did the same as me each Saturday evening. I still didn't fully understand how Jesus fitted into the mix, and every time the minister was about to give a sermon, where my teaching of the Christian faith should have been broadened, a request was made for the children to go out to a small room, where they coloured in pictures. I felt that I was doing my duty by accompanying Natasha, whilst Alison stayed in the worship area to listen to the minister preach, but I was feeling increasingly disappointed, by not hearing what was been said.

During the next two years the church was going through an interregnum, which meant that they were without an appointed vicar for that period of time. I'd managed to get enough visits in to not feel too hypocritical about having Natasha, then Faith, christened, but it became far easier not to attend than to do so, after the ceremonies. Although my stubbornness wouldn't allow me to show much enthusiasm, I began to take note of what Alison had to say about the sermons, genuinely desiring to have a better understanding of what they meant. I would often find booklets lying around the house that were written by RBC Ministries, called Daily Bread, and I found them fascinating as they seemed to tackle difficult subjects head on, with a logical authority that always led back to the Bible. Most of the literature further emphasised the relevance of Jesus' teaching or placed him as importantly as 'Our Father God' or the 'Holy Spirit', and the link between all three parts of the Deity of God, seemed to be slowly falling into place. My Sunday morning lie-in, often in the spare room so as not to disturb the family following my usual Saturday nights` out started to decrease. At the same time, my sense of fulfilment increased when my heart began to reluctantly melt, as the significance and my adoration of Jesus Christ became more evident to me.

For the first time in my life I'd discovered a role model worthy of adulation, but more than that I found myself speaking to him through prayer, sometimes abruptly but mostly reverently, forming a personal relationship that was bringing me to my knees, even though church still seemed relatively insignificant. It was sometime during 1996 that for the first time Alison seemed dismayed with the local church, arriving home slightly despondent that 'no-one ever spoke about God' after the service. This seemed to be the catalyst for her to attend several other churches to see what they had to offer. Challenging Alison about what I was reading or feeling became quite a pastime and it was appropriate timing when she came back from a visit to a church on Deeble Road, Kettering, explaining that it seemed a good match for the whole family to attend.

I always say 'that my heart went before my head' when it came to my conversion, and reading a Daily Bread booklet one evening, I had a most unusual, warm inner feeling in my stomach. The experience gave me immense peace, but was completely different to anything that I'd ever previously encountered. I recall looking at Alison, who was next to me, willing her to say something about this reaction that she may have also been feeling, but she said nothing, leaving me slightly puzzled, even as I quizzed her as to what it might be. I tried passing the experience off as a coincidence, but later recognised it as a time when my heart had said yes to 'Jesus Christ as my Lord and my God,' my trust in Him creating a spiritual awakening and a realisation that I'd been touched significantly by the Holy Spirit.

Sometime later the family attended the 9am service at the modern Anglican church called Christ the King. The building and the service was far from the traditional style that I had been familiar with, and as soon as I walked in the band began to sing songs of praise and worship in a way that I'd never previously heard in a church. The congregation all seemed very friendly, several welcoming us with handshakes, smiles and showing a genuine interest in us and our two children, as we took our place on comfortable, padded seats. However, instead of dreading the number of hymns I had to get through, this time everything was projected onto a large overhead screen and I felt overawed with the words that I was reading or singing to my God, Jesus Christ.

Overwhelmed with emotion, I found myself constantly fighting back tears whilst struggling to deal with the impact the service was having on me. For the first time I heard a sermon that was direct and relevant but explained comprehensively in a way that was easy to listen to, and I was touched deeply inside.

For years I trained hard, achieving high levels of fitness supported by a strong muscular frame, due in part to accommodate the various sports that I participated in. However, it wasn't until I became a Christian that I realised I'd been hiding behind this substantial facade, conforming to people's expectations of me rather than being who I wanted to be. Even in church circles, I found that I was being presented to people as an ex-Northampton Saints player, which disappointed me and became annoying. All I wanted to do was tell people about my conversion to Christianity, and how I'd become a follower of Christ.

This transformation had changed me from the inside out but I realised that it is still okay to have an exciting, competitive edge to my character but with a freedom to pour out love and compassion like I'd never done before. In effect, I'd fallen in love with Jesus Christ and wanted to thank and praise my creator for everything I had. For a while, what I was displaying externally was still very similar to who I'd always been, but my heart was racing as I began to further understand more about who Jesus was. The answers weren't being discovered initially by any deep intellectual or theological study, rather a spiritual discerning to trust what I was reading in scripture as the truth, the written 'Word of God.' Then, as my faith and attitude towards worship developed, so things began to change for the better, and the relevance of church became apparent as I longed to be close to God.

So strong was my sense of calling that I went through the very early stages of discerning whether or not to consider ordination, meeting with the vicar to discuss the way ahead. I was asked to confide in three close friends to pray about the situation, and for several weeks I felt at peace with the thought of being a minister, convincing Alison that it seemed a done deal, only to feel like a fraud a few weeks later as I was seriously challenged by what I was doing.

The thought that I was letting people down came to mind, but I was assured that it was a natural part of the investigation procedure and not to feel too concerned, whatever emotions I was feeling. The time came to meet up with my three friends independently and to find out their thoughts, two of whom were locals and another who'd moved to the East Coast. Remarkably, they all said that they had an overwhelming sense that I should remain in business, and to witness through how I conduct myself in the workplace, something my wife and I did to the best of our ability until selling the company in 2012.

There seemed to be a certain tension in some church circles about businessmen and the whole concept of making money, so I took it upon myself to discuss these and other issues with people I trusted. It was a relief to discover that we are all different, and so are our gifts and talents, but used correctly we can still glorify and honour God with them.

I've had some wonderful experiences serving my church and continue to do so to this day. I can assure anyone that the church is alive and active, you just need to look in the right places like the voluntary sector or community projects, where Christians are often the pioneers behind the cause or involved in the running of the event. To me, my faith is a lifestyle rather than a weekly Sunday meeting and I have found immense freedom in serving others, showing respect, compassion and love in whatever I do. There is a sense of wellbeing, knowing that you are helping people simply because you can and you want to, with no ulterior motives. A case in point was when I served as a Street Pastor. During one Saturday evening, our team of Street Pastor volunteers engaged in conversation with a young man who'd just returned from Jordan, after diving in the Red Sea. A colleague was trying to answer the many religious questions that he threw at her, as he swapped from challenging her first on the Koran, then on her knowledge of the Holy Bible. His aim seemed to be to want to embarrass her about her lack of religious knowledge compared to his. As team leader I stepped in to try and bring the discussion to an appropriate close, commenting on the fact that I'd visited Israel some years previously, and I talked about a rather unfortunate incident when I'd cycled forty miles around Lake Galilee the day before visiting the Dead Sea salt pools. I went on to say that I'd got a sweat rash around my groin area after the long bike ride, and didn't stop to think, before stepping into a heated salt bath. This proved to be a most unwise move as the excruciating pain made me shudder, making my friends scream with laughter, but not as loudly as my screams of pain!

He assumed that because I'd been to Israel I was more religious than the rest of the team, and began talking to me as though I knew every fact that the Bible had to offer. It soon became evident that I knew very little compared to him and he wasn't going to let me off the hook, as his questions came thick and fast. Throughout the discussion I was praying for an answer to some of his questions and a softening of his heart. I trusted that my colleagues were doing the same, when he said, "You're not very religious, are you?" My simple response was "I'm not very religious but I am a man of faith, and I believe that Jesus died for me and that he loves me, just for being who I am."

Although his language was ripe, I believe that the man met with God that evening, as he yelled out loudly "F***g H***l, that's it, that's it, God is love, that's all that matters." He seemed elated, as though a light had been switched on in his mind and heart, as he began shaking our hands excitedly. I had the presence of mind to dig out a New Testament Bible from my rucksack, before saying a discreet prayer with him in the dark streets of Kettering at around midnight on a cool evening. He then ran into the pub with his Bible, shouting to his friends about what had happened to him as we walked off praying and thanking God for our conversation. Incredibly, within five minutes another young man tracked us down and asked if we'd just given a guy a Bible and could he have one too? It turned out that he was a lapsed Christian, who was so overcome with what the other man was saying in the pub, that he felt he needed to say sorry to God and do something about it himself.

The Christian faith is about discovering truth in the Bible, by engaging in a personal relationship with Jesus Christ who then guides us through the Holy Spirit. Without a transformation of character taking place, our faith is fruitless, potentially harmful, and can become stagnant. As a good friend called Melvyn often reminds me: 'God's always got more', so I always seek more, but using God's strength, not my own.

Visiting the Holy Land introduced me head-on to the three main religions of Judaism, Islam and Christianity. In 2000, a group of eight of us toured around Galilee, before moving onto Jerusalem. The commercialism at the tourist sites was almost overwhelming, and the outward expression of piety from those taking care of holy sites, whatever religion, seemed to lack humility. Even at the 'Wailing Wall', as I was about to pray, I was being harassed by an orthodox Jew, asking me to donate money towards his daughter's operation. Later, I engaged with two elderly Jordanian men dressed in traditional dress, and within moments both were condemning Judaism vehemently, after offering indifferent but polite views on Christianity, as if it was of no consequence to them. The Islamic museum, located at Temple Mount and adjacent to the Al-Aqsa mosque, serves as a timely reminder that tensions are just under the surface, and displays of blood-stained clothing, from a massacre in 1990, are permanently left on display. Although having dubious, biblical authenticity, a landscaped garden with an excavated tomb brought a certain peace and tranquillity to my time there. Evangelical Christians manned the site, located next to the city's bus station, and claimed it as Golgotha, or the place of the skull, the spot where Jesus Christ was crucified, prior to being entombed, then resurrected. History, archaeology and many more Christians would definitely dispute this site as being original, but it has an antiquated tomb on site from the era that serves a purpose.

Shortly after my conversion, I had a couple of weeks when my faith was challenged and doubts began to creep in regarding Jesus' resurrection, so to see an authentic tomb and have something tangible to assess, was another answer to prayer. I learnt that the way tombs were sealed, by a heavy, circular entrance stone that fell into place via a hollowed-out track, made it impossible for anything other than a large group of people to move it, and the noise and damage would have been significant in doing so. As I surveyed the site, I was reminded about a revelation that allowed me to fully accept Jesus Christ's resurrection, and his claims of being God during my time of doubt.

Leaving church one Sunday, I was rushing to get Faith back home, but as I strapped her into the car seat, a close friend asked if I could meet him at his house to move a couple of slabs into a skip. I explained that I needed to get back home quickly but that I'd move the slabs by myself. John's facial expression gave away that there was more to the job than I'd anticipated, as he rushed off to tidy up some loose ends in church. I'd been earnestly praying for peace about my resurrection doubts for a few weeks' prior, studying scripture and questioning mature

Christians in the process. When I arrived at the property, I found two slabs propped against the side wall of the garage and a skip parked up on the roadside, some fifteen metres away. With an eternal optimist's enthusiasm, I rushed from my car, quietly shutting the door as Faith, slept. I grabbed one of the slabs and managed to deadlift the stone to just above my ankles, staggering then stumbling no more than a metre, before very nearly collapsing due to the great weight. The slabs were ex-council stock, measuring about three feet by two feet, two inches deep and only a fraction of the weight of a tombstone. Within that moment, as I gasped for air, I believe God revealed to me details about the weight of the entrance stone that someone would have had to move, to steal or hide Jesus' body from the tomb, an impossible task based on the evidence that the Bible supplies. My elation and heartfelt excitement was obvious, as I burst out laughing and thanked God for the revelation, just as my friend John arrived to help me.

Additional biblical testimony where Paul openly challenges anyone to disprove the resurrection, had already helped to allay any remaining doubt or scepticism, and can be found in 1 Corinthians ch.15, v. 1-10.

"Now, brothers and sisters, I want to remind you of the gospel I preached to you, which you received and on which you have taken your stand. ² By this gospel you are saved, if you hold firmly to the word I preached to you. Otherwise, you have believed in vain.³ For what I received I passed on to you as of first importance: that Christ died for our sins according to the Scriptures, ⁴ that he was buried, that he was raised on the third day according to the Scriptures, ⁵ and that he appeared to Cephas, and then to the Twelve. ⁶ After that, he appeared to more than five hundred of the brothers and sisters at the same time, most of whom are still living, though some have fallen asleep. ⁷ Then he appeared to James, then to all the apostles, ⁸ and last of all he appeared to me also, as to one abnormally born.⁹ For I am the least of the apostles and do not even deserve to be called an apostle, because I persecuted the church of God."

Paul then goes on to say, in an emphatic manner, that our faith is futile without the resurrection when he writes the following.

¹⁴ *"And if Christ has not been raised, our preaching is useless and so is your faith. ¹⁵ More than that, we are then found to be false witnesses about God, for we have testified about God that he raised Christ from the dead."*

People come to faith in many different ways and sometimes for many different reasons. Take for instance, Alison's conversion, which was gradual and over many years. However, more than anyone, her devotion to be obedient to Christ's teaching and by having a genuine love for Him led me to find my faith. However, sometimes God has to hit some people harder than others to make them listen! I believe that I was being prepared for the difficulties that lay just around the corner, as within a couple of weeks of committing my life to follow Christ, I received notice that one of our main business clients wanted to visit me. We'd received calls from other contractors, who I knew, ringing to say that this multinational client had threatened some of them with losing their contract if they continued to work for one of their competitors. At the time we benefited from receiving business upwards of £225,000 pa from this main client, but only £25,000 pa with their rival. Although I found it an immoral request, and my initial reaction was one of disbelief, I was convinced that the threat was a serious one and I went home planning to set up another company, so that I could continue trading with both parties, without the major company ever knowing that I was doing so. Alison's response was bold and sermon-like, illogical and reckless from a business viewpoint, reminding me that I'd agreed to follow Christ's teaching, and that we should be standing up to the unethical and immoral practice that this client was enforcing upon us. I argued against her with head knowledge, explaining that I wasn't being deceptive (but really I was), that it was financial suicide to upset them, yet as I spoke, my heart was telling me differently, and I eventually agreed with Alison and decided to challenge their ethics.

A verbal threat was received with a further meeting booked in a week's time for our final decision. So concerned and nervous was I about the outcome that Alison stepped in to lead the discussion, as I tried but failed to record the meeting on a hidden camcorder. Alison's righteous anger put the woman in no doubt as to where we stood, and I don't know who felt more uncomfortable after the short appointment, me or the client. However before she left, the rep did say that we'd totally misunderstood her request that we shouldn't trade with their competitor, saying that business would continue as normal. Business with them did not return to normal and we never received another work order from her company. Due to circumstances that no one could have predicted, we lost two further contracts within four weeks, pushing our loss of income to well over £500,000, a figure that accounted for almost ninety per cent of our total turnover for that year.

For some months previously, I'd felt challenged by a piece of scripture from 1 Timothy ch.6, v.10:

'For the love of money is a root of all kinds of evil. Some people, eager for money, have wandered from the faith and pierced themselves with many griefs.'

I'd misunderstood 'The love of money is a root of all kinds of evil' to read 'Money is the root of all evil.' Examining my motives to make money and praying into the situation, I discovered that I had a healthy respect for it and the many benefits that it can bring, but I didn't love money, which released me from a great burden. This whole process brought me so close to God, as the fear and realisation that we had a potentially bankrupt business on our hands, led me to pray for Him to take it with minimal damage to our staff's livelihoods. Throughout this most uncomfortable period of time, my faith grew immeasurably, even though feeling weak and helpless at times.

My transformation started when I stopped perceiving Jesus as a weak, fragile and powerless person and began reading the Bible and praying for revelation of the truth. Instead, I found Jesus Christ as to be someone who was so tough, yet full of humility, so outraged at injustice, but so compassionate and loving in the way that he deals with atrocious conduct against himself and humanity, a man that became my role model for how to live the rest of my life. To me – and many billions before me – He is our God; to others only a good teacher, someone we choose to ignore, or just a myth. A rapid adjustment was required with the business after losing so much turnover, but a sense of peace stayed with me throughout as I prayed and felt supported by family and close friends from church. However, within several weeks not only had my faith developed but so had the business, when we won contracts that were greater than the amount that we had lost, allowing us to continue trading for many more years to come!

I now attend church regularly, having done so for the last twenty-two years, but with more of an understanding as to why it is important to do so. Ultimately, we are made to worship, praise and glorify 'Our Lord' with everything we have, as Jesus clearly states in Matthew ch.22, v.36-40:

> *"Teacher, which is the greatest commandment in the Law?" Jesus replied: "Love the Lord your God with all your heart and with all your soul and with all your mind.' This is the first and greatest commandment." And the second is like it: 'Love your neighbour as yourself.' All the Law and the Prophets hang on these two commandments."*

Realising what Jesus has done for me, I began to ask what I could do for Him. It was therefore a time when I learnt that there is hope and freedom in following Christ, where whatever I do should be honouring to God, and that he wants me to develop a character that is more like his. I would probably still be filling most of my time striving for self-worth and drinking heavily, if it wasn't for becoming a man of faith. But I've learnt that we all worship and praise something or somebody, and it's apparent to me that we can become enslaved, sometimes heavily burdened by the things that we hold on to too tightly, and those things can quickly become a form of idolatry if we're not careful!

Philippians ch.2, v.1-5 reads

> *Therefore if you have any encouragement from being united with Christ, if any comfort from his love, if any common sharing in the Spirit, if any tenderness and*

compassion, then make my joy complete by being like-minded, having the same love, being one in spirit and of one mind. Do nothing out of selfish ambition or vain conceit. Rather, in humility value others above yourselves, not looking to your own interests but each of you to the interests of the others. In your relationships with one another, have the same mindset as Christ Jesus.'

This piece of scripture tells us what it means to be Christ-like, which isn't a pride-filled, self righteous act but rather a humble act of righteousness (doing what is right or just in God's eyes).

My first return visit to watch Bedford play after retiring from rugby was to a formal luncheon at the ground, and after discovering that I went to church, a friend sarcastically asked me to let him know if I ever found God. All I can say is that this book is my testimony of how I found God when I stopped trying to make Him into something he wasn't, rather than acknowledging what he's already revealed Himself to be, through Jesus Christ. If you haven't already done so, try praying, and ask Jesus to come into your life with a heartfelt desire for him to reveal himself to you, heart to heart and face to face, Amen.

Reviews

A man of great conviction and presence, Glyn Wood was a virtual ever present in the Bedford team that I coached, and which ultimately won promotion at the end of the eighties, to what is now called **The Rugby Premiership**. Utterly honest and reliable, "Woody" belonged to that honourable band of Corinthian rugby players who played "hard but fair". Never one to start trouble, he wouldn't take a backward step should it occur. His powerful carrying and bone crunching tackles could be game-changers, and his larger than life personality made my job a lot easier. Any coach would want characters like Woody in the team.

Richard Chadwick, former coach, Bedford Blues

I thoroughly enjoyed reading the story of your life, and discovered quite a bit about you that I hadn't gleaned beforehand. Here is a very honest portrayal of someone growing up in the sixties and seventies, becoming a high level rugby player (amongst other skills) who is very aware of his own strengths and weaknesses as he makes his way through the navy and into business. Through it all is woven his Christian faith, which is clearly deep rooted and which he seeks to integrate with his daily life – and that chimes with what I know of Glyn. Here is someone whose faith has added colour to a full life giving it a greater sense of purpose and meaning. It is a fascinating story for anyone to read who is involved in the world of sport or the armed forces, which will provoke stimulate and engage them, not least in raising questions about the difference that God can make in a bloke's life. Well worth reading.

Rev'd Mike Talbot. Evangelism Enabler for the Diocese of Carlisle

As a man and as a Christian, Glyn is the real deal – authentic, honest and purposeful. This book is the same – an open window on the story of his life and how faith in Jesus has shaped him.

Rev'd Canon Steve Benoy. Director of Ordinands Vocation and Formation Team for the Diocese of Peterborough